D0604046

BRADLEY'S COMPLETE GAS GRILL COOKBOOK

by Nancy Elmont

Dorison House Publishers   Boston

the author

A professional Home Economist, Nancy Elmont has a degree from Ohio State University. She has worked as a Test Kitchen Director at Kenyon & Eckhardt, Director of Consumer Affairs at Wm. Underwood Co., as well as for hotel, hospital and university food services. She has acted as a consultant and food photography stylist, and has done exclusive home catering in the Boston area. To the delight of family and friends, she enjoys barbecuing wonderful meals in her back yard all summer long.

All rights reserved
including the right of reproduction
in whole or in part in any form.

Copyright 1982
by Dorison House Publishers, Inc.
and W. C. Bradley Enterprises, Inc.

Published by Dorison House Publishers, Inc.
824 Park Square Building
Boston, MA 02116

ISBN: 0916752-54-2   (pbk)

ISBN: 0916752-52-6 (hardcover)

Library of Congress Number: 81-69074

Manufactured in the United States of America

Third Printing, March 1984

contents

introduction

It seems that we Americans have always enjoyed cooking outdoors. From the early cowboys grilling steaks over an open fire, to the lavish Southern plantation barbecues, to the present day backyard cookout, barbecuing has become a favorite national pastime.

Why do we choose to abandon the convenience of the modern kitchen to pursue this peculiarly American style cookery? Meals prepared outdoors are more economical and seem to simply taste better than conventionally prepared meals. More importantly, most of us just plain enjoy relaxing in the fresh air with friends or family around the grill.

Barbecuing should be fun, and that's the whole idea behind *BRADLEY'S COMPLETE GAS GRILL COOKBOOK.*

You have already discovered the hassle-free versatility of the gas grill. And this cookbook contains recipes and helpful hints to even further decrease effort and increase enjoyment.

Start by trying basic steak and hamburger variations like Round Steak Italienne or Hamburgers with Cheese and Herb Filling. Then try your hand at gourmet dishes like Cod Steak with Beurre Blanc, Rotisserie Roasted Leg of Lamb, Chicken Hoisin, or even entire meals prepared on the grill from appetizer to dessert. Tips for outdoor entertaining are also included.

We invite you to use this cookbook as the starting point for your own exploration of the varied and exciting world of outdoor cookery.

getting ready for a barbecue

equipment basics

Cooking on a gas grill becomes as easy as using the range top indoors after a couple of barbecues. With a little practice at lighting, adjusting the flame and timing, you will feel comfortable enough to try almost any food or recipe. It may be smart to begin with basic foods. Try simple hamburgers, hot dogs, steak or chicken before experimenting with more elaborate dishes.

Here's how to begin...

— Check your grill before beginning to cook for the first time to be sure that all parts are assembled correctly and that the gas is properly hooked up.

— Locate the grill away from dry grass, brush and other combustibles. And keep it away from buildings. You may want to check wind direction and relocate the grill depending upon the conditions of the day.

— Before using your grill for the first time, fire up the grill and break it in for 30 minutes before putting the food on to cook. Any odor you notice will be the solvents leaving the high temperature paint finish.

— Preheat the radiant rock for five minutes over a high flame setting with the grill lid closed. The rocks will absorb the heat and provide the radiant heat for broiling and roasting.

accessory musts

Before you can begin, check your selection of utensils and make sure you have

— **mitten-shaped long pot holders**
— **heavy-duty aluminum foil**

    Have foil handy for wrapping foods for the grill and for making drip pans or covers for food on the grill. Be sure to wrap foods with shiny side of foil toward the food.

— **meat thermometer to check temperature of roasts**
— **metal brush for cleaning grill racks**

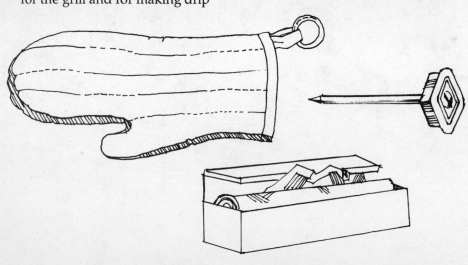

getting ready for a barbecue

6

accessory musts

— **long-handled spatula, fork, and tongs**

All should have insulated handles to keep hands cool near the heat. Remember to use the tongs for turning meats so that you won't lose meat juices.

— **long-handled basting brush**

Select one with natural bristles because the plastic ones may melt.

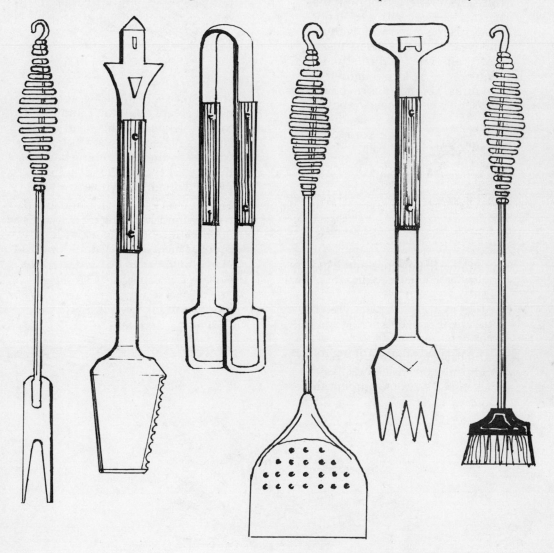

accessory plusses

— A rotisserie offers a deliciously different way to cook on the grill. Roasts, poultry, and game brown and self baste without burning with this useful accessory. When using a rotisserie it is very important that the meat be well balanced. If not, the rotisserie motor will overwork and wear out. For boneless meat, insert rotisserie rod through the center of the meat and tighten the spit forks. For meat with a bone, the rotisserie rod may need to be inserted diagonally to insure proper balance.

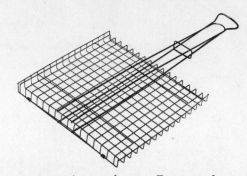

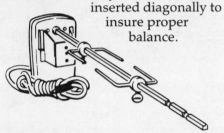

Be sure to tie wings and legs of poultry well when cooking them on a spit.

Ribs may also be placed on the rotisserie if threaded on the spit rod accordian fashion.

— A grill basket simplifies the cooking and turning of small foods like chicken parts, chops, burgers and cut up pieces of meat. Because the basket is hinged, it can be adjusted to the thickness of the meat. For the cooking of fish—either whole, fillets or steaks—there is nothing better than a basket to assure that the pieces will remain whole.

— A Step-Up-Grid expands the grill's cooking and warming capacity. It's a boon to the cook who wants to prepare meat and vegetable or bread at one time. It can be used to warm sauces, heat breads, or simply to grill steaks, burgers, or chops to doneness all at once.

accessory plusses

— Hickory chunks turn any grill into a smoker. They delicately enhance the flavor of meats and fish alike. Be sure to soak chunks in water for an hour or so before using. Then wrap them in foil, puncture foil in several places to allow smoke to escape. Place wrapped chunks onto fire grate and turn grill on high for 15 minutes before cooking or until chunks smolder.

— Metal skewers increase the variety of foods you can prepare on the grill. Select metal skewers that are flat or square so that foods will not roll easily when cooking.

cooking tips

To make cooking easy, here are a few hints for beginners:

— When cooking steaks or roasts, trim away all excess fat to avoid flare-ups.

— When roasting meats or fowl on the grates, place a drip pan directly below the meat on the fire grate to catch fat and juices. Arrange the radiant rock around the drip pan. Use this same procedure when cooking with the rotisserie. See page 12 for instructions on how to make an aluminum foil drip pan.

— For accurate timing, have meats at room temperature before cooking.

— Scent the flavors of meats by sprinkling the radiant rock with fresh or dried herbs which have been soaked in water about an hour before use. Herbs like fennel, tarragon, bay leaves and basil will impart delicate flavors to meat, poultry, and fish.

— Use these cooking methods for meats, poultry and fish:

for steaks and chops, cook over high heat.

for chicken and white meats, use low heat and baste so that meat will not dry.

for fish, select generally the fatty species and those with firm flesh, and cook with a basting sauce so the fish will remain moist.

— To make best use of the grill, cook several items at one time — meats, vegetables and breads.

— On occasion, let guests do their own cooking on the grill. They will have fun grilling their own meal, and you will be free to enjoy your guests.

DIRECT COOKING — Grill on the grate directly over the flames.

TYPE OF FOOD	WEIGHT OR THICKNESS	FLAME SETTING	COOKING TIME		SPECIAL INSTRUCTIONS
Beef			**Rare**	**Medium**	
Burgers	½ inch	Medium to High	7-10 min.	10-15 min.	Grill, turning once
Steaks:	1 inch	Medium to High	8-12 min.	12-20 min.	Remove excess fat, turn once
Filet Mignon, Porterhouse, Rib, Sirloin, Strip, T-Bone, Chuck	1½ inch	Medium to High	11-16 min.	16-25 min.	Remove excess fat, turn once
Roasts		Low	20-25 min. (per lb.)	25-30 min. (per lb.)	Use foil pan
Tenderloin	4-6 lbs.	High	30-40 min.		Remove surface fat, bind with string
Pork / Ham				**Well Done**	
Ham Steaks	½ inch	High		12-15 min.	Remove excess fat, turn once
Chops	½ inch	Medium		20-40 min.	Remove excess fat, turn frequently
	1 inch	Medium		35-60 min.	Remove excess fat, turn frequently
Ribs	5-6 lbs.	Medium		45-60 min.	Turn occasionally
Roast	4-5 lbs.	Low		1¾-2¼ hrs.	Use foil pan
Ham	3-5 lbs.	Low		35 min.	Turn once
Poultry				**Well done**	
Chicken-Halved or quartered		Low to Medium		40-60 min.	Turn frequently, use foil pan
Chicken-Whole	2-3 lbs	Low		1½-1¾ hrs.	Use foil pan
Turkey	5-8 lbs.	Low		25-30 min. (per lb.)	Use a foil pan, meat thermometer inserted in thigh should read 185°F.
Seafood				**Well Done**	
Fillets	6-8 ounces	Medium to High		8-12 min.	Turn once
Steaks	¾ to 1 inch	Medium to High		8-15 min.	Turn once
Whole	4-8 ounces	Medium to High		12-20 min.	Turn once
Shrimp	Large	Low		18-22 min.	Turn once

cooking times and temperatures

INDIRECT COOKING — Dual burner models allow indirect cooking. Ignite one side of burner and place food on other side for slow cooking.

TYPE OF FOOD	WEIGHT OR THICKNESS	FLAME SETTING	COOKING TIME IN COVERED GRILL		SPECIAL INSTRUCTIONS
			Rare	Medium	
Beef Roast	4-6 lbs.	Medium	1-1¼ hrs.	1¼-1½ hrs.	Use a foil pan
				Well Done	
Pork Roast	4-5 lbs.	Medium		2½ hrs.	Internal temperature-170°F
Ham	3-5 lbs.	Medium		¾ hr.	
	9-10 lbs.	Medium		1-1¼ hrs.	
Chicken-Whole	3-4 lbs.	Low to Medium		¾-1 hr.	Use a foil pan
Turkey (unstuffed)	5-8 lbs.	Medium		1¾-2¼ hrs.	Use a foil pan
Duck (Domestic)	3-5 lbs.	Medium		¾-1¼ hrs.	Use a foil pan

ROTISSERIE COOKING

TYPE OF FOOD	WEIGHT OR THICKNESS	FLAME SETTING	COOKING TIME		SPECIAL INSTRUCTIONS
			Rare	Medium	
Beef Roast	4-6 lbs.	Low to Medium	2-2½ hrs.	2½-3 hrs.	Use a foil pan
				Well Done	
Pork Roast	4-5 lbs.	Low to Medium		1¼-1½ hrs.	Use a foil pan, internal temperature-170°F
Ham	3-5 lbs.	Low		½-¾ hr.	Use a foil pan
Chicken-Whole	2-3 lbs.	Low to Medium		1½-2½ hrs.	Use a foil pan, secure legs and wings
Game Hens	1-1½ lbs.	Medium to High		1-1½ hrs.	Use a foil pan, secure legs and wings
Turkey	5-8 lbs.	Low to Medium		2-2½ hrs.	Use a foil pan, secure legs and wings
Duck (Domestic)	3-5 lbs.	Low to Medium		2-3½ hrs.	Use a foil pan, secure legs and wings

how to make an aluminum foil drip pan

Use a foil drip pan when grilling either foods that require frequent basting with oil or contain a significant amount of fat. By following these simple instructions, you can prevent annoying flare-ups.

1. Use double sheet of 18″ heavy-duty aluminum foil which will extend at least 3″ beyond each end of meat.
2. Fold all edges over about 1½″ to 2″.
3. Flatten down all folds as in Diagram

No. 3 and turn the entire sheet over.

4. Using your fingernail, score all the way around 1″ from the edge and diagonally from the corners through the point where the scores intersect.
5. Fold all edges up and pull out the four corners. Pinch these corners as in Diagram No. 5.
6. Fold corners back against sides and pinch as shown in diagram No. 6.

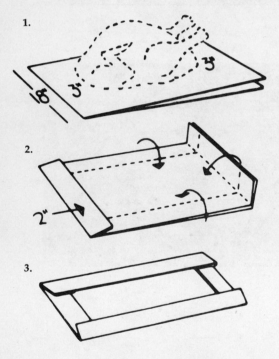

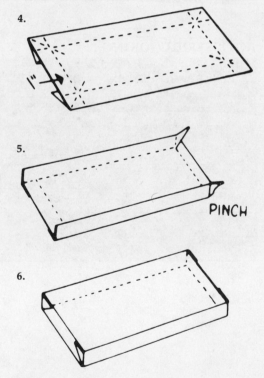

care of the gas grill

Cast Iron Cooking Grates

Cast iron has been used many years for cooking purposes and is still preferred by better chefs throughout the country. Following these time-tested instructions for the care of your cast iron grates should insure years of rust-free service:

— Before first use, wet grates in warm water and scrub with mild cleanser and cloth. Remove all cleanser with hot water. Thoroughly dry and cover grates with generous coat of cooking oil.

— Heat stove oven to 350°F. Place grates on large rimmed cookie sheets or baking pans to prevent oil from dripping in oven.

— Leave grates in oven for 2 to 3 hours. Turn off oven, remove grates and allow to cool enough to handle. Rub again with cooking oil. Wipe off excess with paper towel. Your grates are now "seasoned."

— After each use, turn gas off. While the grates are still warm, loosen cooking residue with stiff brush and wipe clean with paper towel. Rub with thin coat of cooking oil. Do not clean grates by "burning off" at high temperatures.

— Like all cast iron, water or moisture will cause the grates to rust. If you keep the grates properly "seasoned" this should not happen. If you do not use your grill often, we recommend storing grates indoors in a dry place.

---

getting ready for a barbecue

care of the gas grill

Chrome Wire Cooking Grates

Before each cookout, apply a light coating of cooking oil to chrome wire grates. This helps prevent sticking foods. Chrome wire grates may be washed. Dry thoroughly and store indoors between cookouts.

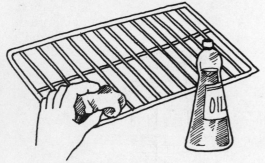

Radiant Rock

To prevent excessive grease accumulation, it is necessary to clean the rock occasionally. You may boil rock in a large container with a tablespoon or so of low sudsing dish washing detergent for 1 hour and rinse thoroughly. Dry rock completely before returning to the grill.

Burner

The grill is equipped with an H-shaped stainless steel burner. Occassionally it is necessary to remove the burner from the grill and clean it. Brush it with a wire brush to remove residue. Check gas ports; if they are clogged, it will be necessary to push a small wire through the ports to open them. The extreme high heat of the grill will eventually, dissipate the chrome in the stainless, causing it to corrode and so the burner will eventually have to be replaced.

Grill Interior

Remove grates, rock and burner from grill to clean. Loosen cooking residues from sides and bottom of grill with a scraper or putty knife. Wipe away loose material with paper towels.

storage of the gas grill

If the grill is to be stored for winter or any length of time, follow these steps:

— Wipe cooking grates clean and oil with cooking oil

— Wrap cooking grates in paper towels and store indoors in a dry location

— The burner should be cleaned, oiled lightly, wrapped in paper towels and stored indoors.

— Store the LP tank OUTSIDE with the valve knob removed. Store the LP tank knob out of the reach of children.

— The valve orifice of the grill should be covered in aluminum foil or protected with tape to prevent small insects from entering during storage.

— The grill should be covered if it is to be left outdoors, using a cover which is available as an accessory.

— Any wooden side shelves should be washed, dried, coated with mineral oil and stored indoors.

Refinishing

After extended use and exposure to the weather, the paint on your grill will deteriorate and may become white spotted. You may refinish the grill if you wish the following way:

— Brush top and bottom with wire brush. Using fine grit sand paper, lightly sand grill so new paint will adhere to the old.

— Wash with soap and water to remove dust and grease. Wipe with vinegar to remove white corrosion.

— Refinish with heat resistant grill paint.

planning an outdoor barbecue party

Although you'll enjoy using your grill year 'round, outdoor entertaining is delightful in warm pleasant weather. And with a gas grill, the barbecue chef can enjoy the party while tending the meal.

Hopefully, you'll be blessed with pleasant weather for your cookout. To help control bothersome insects, try placing special candles on tables, spraying the yard before guests arrive, or using an electric bug killer.

If the day looks promising, set the tables long before the barbecue begins. The table top decor should take its cue from the type of party you are planning. A simple family gathering or casual party might call for paper plates, napkins, and table clothes. For a special occasion, you may want to break out the table linen, good glasses, and flatware. Whatever the occasion, bright colors go well with outdoor dining.

If you intend to serve the meal outside, plan on extra tables for serving platters, beverage pitchers, or serving utensils. Or you might rather serve the meal buffet style indoors even though guests will be seated outdoors.

Be sure to plan for an adequate area to place appetizers, set up a bar, etc.

When planning a menu, select dishes with variety in color, flavor, and texture. Preparing as many items on the grill as possible will allow you to spend more time outside with your guests.

On pages 18 to 20, that follow, we've provided a few favorite menus using recipes that you'll find in this book.

suggested menus

Lime Grilled Chicken (page 70)
Stuffed Artichokes (page 112)
Green and Wax Beans with Onion (page 106)

Seasonal Salad (page 120)

Marshmallow Baked Apples (page 136)

Steamed Mussels (page 98)

Marinated Butterflied Lamb (page 82)
Potato Slices in Foil (page 106)
Cherry Tomatoes with Basil (page 109)

Feta Pocket Bread (page 114)

Praline-Chocolate Ice Cream Bombe (page 130)

Anchovy Mayonnaise with Crudités (page 22)

Rotisserie Peppered Eye of the Round (page 47)
Au Gratin Potatoes (page 104)
Squash Kebobs with Garlic Butter (page 110)

Fennel Bread (page 113)

Strawberries with Cassis Sabayon (page 129)

suggested menus

Buttermilk Cucumber Soup (page 28)

Salmon with mustard Dill Sauce (page 95)
Corn with Green Onion (page 107)
Sweet and Sour Beets (page 124)

Toasted Bread Sticks (page 115)

Coconut Toasted Pound Cake (page 134)

suggested menus

Old-fashioned Spareribs (page 59)
Baked Stuffed Potatoes (page 105)
Shredded Zucchini Salad (page 123)

Italian Toasted Muffins (page 115)

Banana Boats (page 137)

Ground Beef Roll-Ups (page 40)
Grilled Eggplant with Garlic (page 108)
Mushrooms on Skewer (page 110)

Double Chocolate Cake (page 133)

Orange Bourbon Pork Chops(page 55)
Grilled Onions (page 111)
Marinated Chinese Vegetable Salad (page 126)

Floating Islands in Jamoca Cream (page 138)

eggplant-onion spread

Chilled eggplant spread is a simple dish to serve because the work is done hours before guests arrive.

1	large eggplant (1½ lbs.)
4	large onions, finely chopped
¼ lb.	butter or margarine
1	green pepper, finely chopped
2 tablespoons	dried dill weed
1 tablespoon	lemon juice
1 tablespoon	sugar
1 can (6 oz.)	tomato paste
2 tablespoons	vegetable oil
1 teaspoon	salt
¼ teaspoon	ground pepper
	sour cream

Prick eggplant in several places with fork and cook on grill over low heat, turning regularly, for about 30 minutes or until skin will peel off easily; cool. Peel skin from eggplant. Chop eggplant very finely. In a fry pan over moderate heat, cook onion in butter until soft. Add eggplant, green pepper, dill, lemon juice, sugar, tomato paste, oil, salt and pepper; remove from heat. Spoon mixture into well-greased 1 quart casserole and bake, uncovered, at 350° F. for 1 hour. Remove from oven and chill. To serve, garnish with dollops of sour cream. Serve with toast rounds.

Makes 10-12 servings as an appetizer.

anchovy mayonnaise with crudités

Homemade mayonnaise is embellished with anchovy fillets.

1	egg
4 tablespoons	lemon juice
2 teaspoons	prepared mustard
¾ cup	vegetable oil
4	anchovy fillets
	ready-to-eat fresh vegetables (cucumber spears, green pepper slices, cherry tomatoes, raw mushrooms, carrot sticks)

In cup of blender or food processor, beat together egg, lemon juice and mustard. Very gradually beat in oil. Add anchovies and purée. Pour mixture into small serving bowl. Serve with chilled raw vegetables.

Makes 4 servings.

deviled shrimp

The same marinade could be used for mussels, scallops or other seafood.

1½ lbs.	medium raw shrimp, peeled
¾ cup	vegetable oil
6 tablespoons	lemon juice
1 tablespoon	prepared Dijon mustard
¾ teaspoon	salt
½ teaspoon	ground pepper
½ teaspoon	instant minced garlic
	lettuce leaves

Cook shrimp in rapidly boiling salted water for 3-5 minutes or until tender. Drain and cool. Meanwhile, in a bowl, stir together oil, lemon juice, mustard, salt, pepper and garlic. Place cooled shrimp in seasoned oil and toss until shrimp are well coated. Cover bowl and chill. Allow to marinate for at least 3-4 hours. Before serving, toss again in marinade. To serve, spoon drained shrimp onto lettuce leaves.

Makes 6 servings as hors d'oeuvre or first course.

scallops seviche

*The scallops are "cooked" by marinating for several hours
in a seasoned lemon-lime juice.*

1	medium tomato, peeled, seeded and chopped
¼ cup	finely chopped onion
1 can (4 oz.)	whole green chilies, seeded, chopped and drained
⅓ cup	lemon juice
⅓ cup	lime juice
½ teaspoon	salt
¼ teaspoon	ground cumin
⅛ teaspoon	ground pepper
1 lb.	fresh scallops

In a bowl, stir together tomato, onion, chilies, lemon juice, lime juice, salt, cumin and pepper. Add scallops and stir well to coat. Cover and refrigerate for at least 6 hours, stirring 2 or 3 times during marinating. Serve on lettuce.

Makes 6 servings.

sautéed almonds

This simple hors d'oeuvre can be cooked just before guests arrive so that the almonds can cool off a bit before serving.

5 oz.	whole almonds
1 tablespoon	vegetable oil
¼ teaspoon	instant minced garlic
¼ teaspoon	salt
½ teaspoon	celery salt
¼ teaspoon	coarsely ground pepper
	aluminum foil

Make a small rectangular aluminum foil pan from double thickness of foil. Place almonds, oil, garlic, salts and pepper in foil pan and toss. Place pan over high heat on grill and cook, stirring frequently for about 5 minutes or until almonds are toasted. Cool.

Makes 1 cup flavored almonds.

cheese-topped loaves

For variety, use the same cheese spread on different kinds of bread.

2 packages (3 oz., each)	cream cheese, softened
½ lb.	Muenster cheese, shredded
¼ cup	grated Parmesan cheese
¼ cup	minced scallion
½ teaspoon	chili powder
½ loaf	French bread
	aluminum foil

In a bowl, beat together cheeses, scallion and chili powder. Cut French bread horizontally and spread with cheese mixture. Wrap each piece of bread separately in aluminum foil and place on Step-Up-Grid over low heat in covered grill. Warm for 10-15 minutes. Slice warmed bread into 2-inch pieces.

Makes 4-6 servings as appetizer.

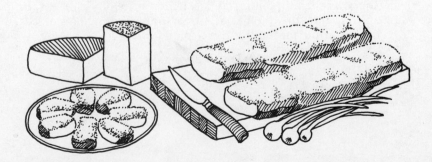

plum-port chicken drummers

Chicken drummers are the large portion of the chicken wing. If you wish, use the entire chicken wing.

⅔ cup	plum jam
¼ cup	port wine
1 tablespoon	lemon juice
1 tablespoon	slivered lemon rind
1 lb. (14)	chicken drummers

In a bowl, stir together jam, wine, lemon juice and rind. Add chicken drummers and stir until chicken is coated. Cover and allow to stand, refrigerated, for 1-2 hours. Cook over low heat in covered grill for about 20 minutes or until done.

Makes 4-5 servings as hors d'oeuvre.

cocktail franks with mustard sauce

Here's a simple way to dress up cocktail franks.

1 lb.	cocktail franks
	metal or wooden skewers
¼ cup	vegetable oil
4 teaspoons	soy sauce
2 tablespoons	prepared mustard

Arrange franks on skewers. In a small bowl, beat together oil, soy and mustard. Place franks on grill over medium heat. Baste with mustard mixture. Cook for 5-8 minutes, turning and basting periodically.

Makes 6-8 servings as appetizer.

white wine fizz

Simple and refreshing — truly a summer beverage.

1	lemon, cut into 6 wedges
1 bottle	medium dry white wine, chilled
1 quart	soda water, chilled
	ice cubes

Squeeze a lemon wedge and place lemon into 6 tall glasses. Pour wine and then club soda into each glass. Stir. Add ice; stir again and serve.

Makes 6 servings.

white wine sangria

Here's the fresh fruit taste of sangria with a new color.

1 bottle	medium dry white wine
2 tablespoons	superfine sugar
2	lemons, thinly sliced
2	oranges, thinly sliced
	ice cubes

Pour wine into pitcher. Add sugar and stir. Squeeze lemons and oranges into wine and put fruit into pitcher. Add ice cubes and stir again.

Makes 4-6 servings.

rosy fruit punch

For decorative ice cubes, freeze small orange segments with water in ice trays.

1 can (12 oz.)	frozen lemonade, defrosted
1 bottle (32 oz.)	cranberry juice cocktail, chilled
1 cup	orange juice
1	orange, thinly sliced
1	lemon, thinly sliced
	ice

Reconstitute lemonade according to package directions. In a large bowl or pitcher, stir together lemonade, cranberry juice cocktail and orange juice. Squeeze orange and lemon slices into fruit juices and put fruit into liquid. Stir well. Pour into tall glasses filled with ice.

Makes 10-12 servings.

fruit daiquiri

Select the fruit flavor for this drink based on what is in season, or simply by your favorite flavor.

1 cup	fruit purée (banana, strawberry or peach)
¼ cup	fresh lime juice
2 tablespoons	superfine or confectioners' sugar
⅓ cup	light rum
4 cups	shaved or cracked ice

In cup of blender, whir together fruit purée, lime juice, sugar, rum and ice. Pour into 4 wine glasses.

Makes 4 servings.

piña colada

Garnish this beverage with a fresh pineapple slice.

⅓ cup	cream of coconut
1½ cups	pineapple juice
¾ cup	dark rum
2 cups	cracked or crushed ice

Pour cream of coconut, pineapple juice, rum and ice into cup of blender. Whir until ingredients are well blended. Pour into tall glasses to serve.

Makes 4-6 servings.

fresh melon soup

This recipe calls for cantaloupe though any favorite melon would make a delicious soup.

4 cups	cut up cantaloupe
1 cup	orange juice
¼ cup	light cream
¼ cup	lemon juice
¼ teaspoon	grated lemon rind

Place all ingredients in cup of blender or food processor; purée. Chill thoroughly before serving. To serve, garnish with a few pieces of cut up melon or a sprig of mint.

Makes 4 servings.

chilly buttermilk cucumber soup

Before serving give this soup a few hours to sit in the refrigerator to let the flavors blend.

2	medium cucumbers, peeled
4 cups	buttermilk
2 cups	sour cream
1	small onion, grated
1 teaspoon	salt
3 drops	hot red pepper sauce
3 tablespoons	chopped parsley, divided

Cut cucumbers horizontally and scoop out seeds. Cut cucumber into chunks and place in cup of blender; purée. Put purée in bowl and stir in buttermilk, sour cream, onion, salt, pepper sauce and 2 tablespoons parsley; mix thoroughly. Cover and refrigerate. Garnish with additional parsley when serving.

Makes 6-8 servings.

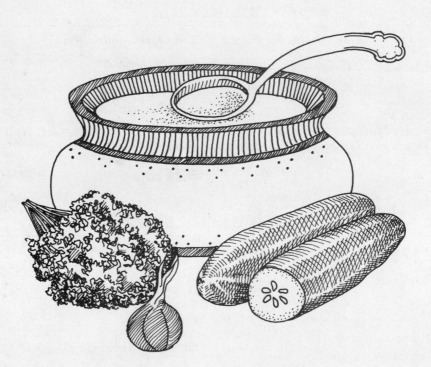

delicious main dishes

beef

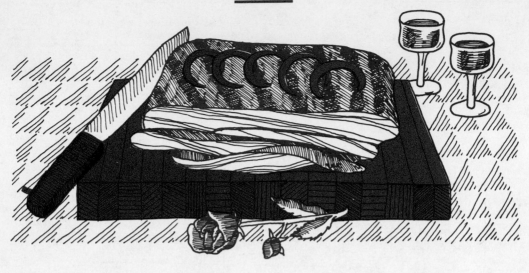

basic burgers

Here's the simplest — just ground beef, salt and pepper.

2 lbs.	ground beef
1½ teaspoons	salt
½ teaspoon	ground pepper

Mix meat lightly with salt and pepper in a bowl. Shape into 8 patties. Place on grill over medium to high heat. Cook on each side for about 5 minutes.

For more interesting burgers, try your hand at a variety of fillings, bastes and toppings. For each serving, divide meat into two patties, making a raised rim of meat around the edge of one patty. Place some filling on top of the patty with the raised edge and cover with flat meat patty. Seal two patties together to hold in filling. Cook to desired degree of doneness. In fact, let family and friends enjoy making their own favorite combinations when you set out bowls full of ingredients.

Here are a few suggestions:

delicious main dishes

cheese and herb filling

1 cup	shredded mozzarella cheese
¾ teaspoon	fennel seed, crushed
1 teaspoon	dried marjoram leaves
⅛ teaspoon	ground pepper

In a bowl, stir together cheese, fennel, marjoram and pepper.

Makes filling for 6 burgers.

zippy pineapple filling

1 can (7¾ oz.)	crushed pineapple, drained
½ teaspoon	dry mustard
¼ teaspoon	ground clove

In a bowl, stir together pineapple, mustard and clove.

Makes filling for 6 burgers.

tomato and olive filling

1	medium onion, finely chopped
1 tablespoon	vegetable oil
3	medium tomatoes, peeled, seeded and coarsely chopped
⅓ cup	finely chopped stuffed olives
¼ teaspoon	salt

In a small fry pan, sauté onion in oil over moderate heat until tender. Add tomatoes and cook for 3-5 minutes. Remove from heat and stir in olives and salt.

Makes filling for 6 burgers.

blue cheese filling

1 cup (4 oz.)	crumbled Danish blue cheese
2 tablespoons	lemon juice
1½ teaspoons	grated lemon rind
⅛ teaspoon	ground pepper

In a bowl, stir together cheese, lemon juice, lemon rind and pepper until smooth.

Makes filling for 6 burgers.

mushroom-wine filling

3 cups	sliced fresh mushrooms
3 tablespoons	butter or margarine
3 tablespoons	dry vermouth
1½ teaspoons	lemon juice
1 tablespoon	chopped parsley
½ teaspoon	salt
⅛ teaspoon	ground pepper

In a fry pan, sauté mushrooms in butter over moderate heat. When mushrooms are tender, pour in vermouth, lemon juice, parsley, salt and pepper. Cook for 3-5 minutes; cool.

Makes filling for 6 burgers.

bacon chive filling

2 tablespoons	crumbled cooked bacon
¼ cup	minced chives

In a small bowl, stir together bacon and chives.

Makes filling for 6 burgers.

oriental filling

¾ cup	chopped scallion
2 tablespoons	butter or margarine
¾ cup	chopped water chestnuts
⅛ teaspoon	salt
dash	ground pepper

In a small fry pan, sauté scallion in butter over moderate heat until scallion is soft. Remove from heat and stir in water chestnuts, salt and pepper.

Makes filling for 6 burgers.

pork sausage filling

¼ lb.   bulk pork sausage
⅓ cup   chopped celery
1 tablespoon chopped parsley

In a small fry pan, cook sausage over moderate heat until well browned. Stir in celery and parsley; cook for an additional 5 minutes. Drain and cool.

Makes filling for 6 burgers.

lemon greek baste

½ cup   vegetable oil
4 tablespoons lemon juice
1½ teaspoons minced fresh mint
½ teaspoon   dried leaf oregano
½ teaspoon   salt
⅛ teaspoon   ground pepper

In a bowl, stir together oil, lemon juice, mint, oregano, salt and pepper. With a brush, baste on burgers or other meats.

Makes about ¾ cup baste.

garlic italian baste

½ cup   vegetable oil
3 tablespoons red wine vinegar
2   garlic cloves, minced
½ teaspoon   dried basil leaves
½ teaspoon   dried oregano leaves
1 teaspoon   salt
¼ teaspoon   ground pepper

In a bowl, stir together oil, vinegar, garlic, basil, oregano, salt and pepper. With a brush, baste on burgers or other meats.

Makes about ¾ cup baste.

cider-ginger baste

1 can (6 oz.)	concentrated frozen apple juice
¼ teaspoon	grated fresh ginger root

In a bowl, stir together apple juice and ginger. With a brush, baste on burgers or other meats.

Makes about ¾ cup baste.

ranchero baste

1 tablespoon	vegetable oil
1	large onion, chopped
2	garlic cloves, minced
1 teaspoon	dried oregano leaves
1 teaspoon	dried basil leaves
⅛ teaspoon	crushed red pepper
1 can (15 oz.)	tomato sauce

In a fry pan, heat oil. Over moderate heat, cook onion and garlic until soft, not browned. Stir in oregano, basil, pepper and tomato sauce. Allow to simmer for 20-30 minutes. With a brush, baste on burgers and other meats.

Makes about 1½ cups baste.

soy sherry baste

¼ cup	soy sauce
¼ cup	medium dry sherry
6 tablespoons	light corn syrup
1 teaspoon	ground fresh ginger root

In a bowl, stir together soy sauce, sherry, corn syrup and ginger. With a brush, baste on burgers and other meats.

wine baste

¾ cup	red wine
1	garlic clove, minced
2 tablespoons	vegetable oil
¾ teaspoon	salt
½ teaspoon	dried thyme leaves
¼ teaspoon	dried rosemary leaves
¼ teaspoon	ground pepper

In a bowl, stir together wine, garlic, oil, salt, thyme, rosemary and pepper. With a brush, baste on burgers and other meats.

Makes about 1 cup.

creamy cheddar topping

1 cup	shredded sharp cheddar cheese
1 package (3 oz.)	cream cheese, softened
⅓ cup	milk
¼ teaspoon	ground pepper
	yellow food coloring

In cup of blender or food processor, blend cheeses, milk, pepper and coloring.

Makes about 1½ cups.

louis topping

¾ cup	mayonnaise
2½ tablespoons	chili sauce
1 tablespoon	prepared horseradish
1 teaspoon	lemon juice

In a bowl, stir together mayonnaise, chili sauce, horseradish and lemon juice. Chill and serve.

Makes about 1 cup.

horseradish topping

1 cup	sour cream
2½ teaspoons	prepared horseradish
¼ teaspoon	salt

In a bowl, stir together sour cream, horseradish and salt. Chill and serve.

Makes about 1 cup.

guacamole topping

1	ripe avocado, peeled
1 tablespoon	lemon juice
1 tablespoon	minced onion
¼ teaspoon	salt
3 drops	hot red pepper sauce

In a bowl, mash avocado. Stir in lemon juice, onion, salt and pepper sauce. Cover and chill thoroughly.

Makes about ¾ cup.

tangy mustard topping

¾ cup	mayonnaise
2 tablespoons	Dijon mustard
¾ teaspoon	dried tarragon leaves

In a bowl, stir together mayonnaise, mustard and tarragon. Cover and chill.

Makes about 1 cup.

snappy chili topping

2 tablespoons	vegetable oil
1	onion, chopped
1	garlic clove, minced
1 can (15 oz.)	tomato sauce
1 can (16 oz.)	kidney beans, drained
2 teaspoons	chili powder
¾ teaspoon	ground cumin
½ teaspoon	dried oregano leaves

Over moderate temperature, heat oil in fry pan. Add onions and garlic; cook until onions are tender, not browned. Add tomato sauce, kidney beans, chili powder, cumin and oregano. Continue to cook for 30 minutes. Cool. Spoon over burgers.

Makes about 2 cups.

delicious main dishes

BEEF CHART

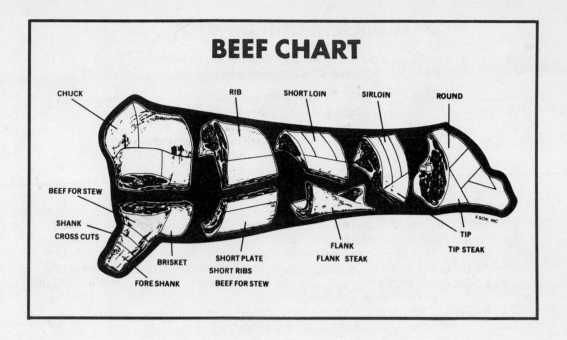

CHUCK · RIB · SHORT LOIN · SIRLOIN · ROUND

BEEF FOR STEW

SHANK
CROSS CUTS

BRISKET

SHORT PLATE
SHORT RIBS

FORE SHANK

BEEF FOR STEW

FLANK
FLANK STEAK

TIP
TIP STEAK

© SCW. INC

sausage and beef burgers

Pork sausage makes these into extra spicy burgers.

1 lb.	ground beef
8 oz.	bulk pork sausage
1	egg, slightly beaten
¾ cup	fine, dry bread crumbs
2 tablespoons	minced onion

In a bowl, stir together beef, sausage, egg, crumbs and onion. Shape into 6 patties. Place on grill over medium heat. Cover grill and cook for about 10 minutes per side.

Makes 6 servings.

sweet and sour meatballs

So that the sauce will not burn as meatballs cook, save the basting for the last 10 minutes of barbecuing.

½ cup	catsup, divided
5 tablespoons	cider vinegar
2 tablespoons	brown sugar
1	small onion, finely chopped
½ teaspoon	ground pepper, divided
1 lb.	ground beef
1	egg
1 teaspoon	salt

In a saucepan, stir together catsup, vinegar, brown sugar, onion and ¼ teaspoon pepper. Bring to simmer over low heat and cook for 20-25 minutes. Meanwhile, in a bowl, stir together beef, egg, salt and remaining pepper. Shape into about 1 dozen meatballs. Place meatballs on grill over low heat. Cook in covered grill for about 20 minutes, turning periodically. Baste with sweet and sour sauce and continue cooking and turning for an additional 10 minutes.

Makes 4 servings.

meatballs with cheddar baste

Especially good when served on an herbed rice with a crisp green salad.

½ can (11 oz.)	condensed cheddar cheese soup
6 tablespoons	milk
1	medium onion, finely chopped
¼ cup	chopped green pepper
1 teaspoon	Worcestershire sauce
1 lb.	ground beef
1	egg, slightly beaten
¼ cup	fine, dry bread crumbs
½ teaspoon	salt
¼ teaspoon	ground pepper
	metal or wooden skewers

In a bowl, beat together soup with milk. When smooth, stir in onion, green pepper and Worcestershire sauce. In another bowl, stir together ground beef, egg, bread crumbs, salt and pepper. Shape into 15-20 meatballs. Arrange meatballs on skewers and place on grill. Baste with cheddar sauce. Cook over low heat in covered grill for about 20 minutes, turning and basting periodically during cooking.

Makes 4-6 servings.

mini meat loaves

To make cooking simpler, meat loaves may be cooked in the grill basket.

2 lbs.	ground beef
1¼ cups	crushed onion-flavored crackers
1	egg, slightly beaten
1 teaspoon	salt
¼ teaspoon	ground pepper
¼ cup	catsup
2 tablespoons	beef broth
1 tablespoon	soy sauce
1 teaspoon	prepared mustard
2 tablespoons	minced onion

In a bowl, stir together beef, cracker crumbs, egg, salt and pepper. Shape into 6 loaves or rectangular burgers. Place on grill. In a small bowl, stir together catsup, broth, soy sauce, mustard and minced onion. Cook loaves over medium heat in covered grill for about 15 minutes, turning once. Baste with sauce and continue cooking, turning and basting occasionally for another 10 minutes.

Makes 6 servings.

kebob-a-bobs

Known by many names, this Middle Eastern specialty derives its distinctive flavor from the use of bulghur or cracked wheat.

½ cup	fine bulghur wheat
1 lb.	ground beef
1	small onion, finely chopped
2	garlic cloves, finely minced
1 tablespoon	chopped parsley
1½ teaspoon	salt
	metal or wooden skewers

In a small bowl, soak bulghur wheat for 5 minutes in cool water to cover. In a large bowl, stir together beef, onion, garlic, parsley, salt and bulghur; mix thoroughly. Divide meat into 8 equal parts; pat each into sausage shape. Place skewer through center of each "sausage." Place meat on grill rack over low heat. Cook covered for 10-15 minutes, turning periodically.

Makes 4 servings.

ground beef roll-ups

By using a selection of green and red peppers, you'll create a very colorful dish.

1½ lbs.	ground beef
¼ cup	fine dry bread crumbs
2 tablespoons	catsup
1	egg
2	medium onions, thinly sliced
2	green peppers, seeded and thinly sliced
2 tablespoons	vegetable oil
¼ cup	grated Parmesan cheese
8	bacon strips
	food picks

In a bowl, stir together beef, crumbs, catsup and egg; set aside. In a fry pan, cook onions and peppers in vegetable oil over moderate heat until tender, not browned. On a piece of waxed paper or foil, pat meat out into a rectangle 11-inches by 16-inches. Spread onion-pepper mixture evenly over meat. Sprinkle with cheese. Roll up meat, jelly roll fashion, beginning with long side. Slice meat roll into 8 pieces. Wrap each piece with bacon strip; secure bacon strip with food pick. Place roll-ups on grill over low to medium heat and cook in covered grill for about 20 minutes, turning once during cooking.

Makes 8 servings.

stuffed zucchini mozzarella

This recipe is especially good at the end of the summer growing season when zucchini are abundant.

½ cup	chopped onion
½ cup	chopped celery
1	garlic clove, minced
3 tablespoons	vegetable oil
1 lb.	ground beef
1 cup	cooked rice
2 tablespoons	tomato paste
1¼ teaspoon	salt
1 teaspoon	dried oregano leaves
¼ teaspoon	ground pepper
6-8	medium zucchini
1 cup	shredded mozzarella cheese
	aluminum foil

In a fry pan over moderate heat, cook onion, celery and garlic in oil. When tender, add beef and continue cooking until meat is browned. Stir in rice, tomato paste, salt, oregano and pepper. Remove from heat. Cut zucchini in half lengthwise. Scoop out and discard seeds from zucchini halves, leaving thick shells for stuffing. Place zucchini halves in metal baking pan. Pile meat filling into shells and top with cheese. Cover pan with foil, sealing well. Place pan on grill over low heat. Close grill and cook for about 30 minutes.

Makes 6-8 servings.

marinated cube steaks

These steaks can be served as is or can be made into steak sandwiches.

⅓ cup	vegetable oil
2 tablespoons	red wine vinegar
2 tablespoons	soy sauce
1 tablespoon	steak sauce
1	garlic clove, minced
1½ teaspoons	salt
1½ lbs.	cube steaks

In a bowl, stir together oil, vinegar, soy, steak sauce, garlic and salt. Pour into plastic bag. Place meat in bag and seal well. Turn bag so that meat is well coated with marinade. Marinate for 2 hours at room temperature or 4 hours refrigerated. Remove meat from marinade and place on grill over high heat. Cook for about 5 minutes per side, basting periodically with marinade.

Makes 4-6 servings.

mexican marinated steak

A zesty, but not overly hot marinade for beef.

1 can (4 oz.)	whole green chilies
1 can (8 oz.)	tomato sauce
3 tablespoons	lemon juice
1	small onion, peeled
1 teaspoon	dried coriander leaves
3 drops	hot red pepper sauce
1	beef steak (porterhouse, sirloin, london broil), cut 1½ inches thick (about 2 lbs.)

In cup of blender or food processor, purée chilies, tomato sauce, lemon juice, onion, coriander and pepper sauce. Place steak in large plastic bag. Pour tomato sauce purée over steak. Seal bag well and turn so that meat is well coated. Marinate, refrigerated, for about 4 hours. Cook on grill over medium to high heat for about 6-8 minutes per side, basting periodically with marinade. Adjust cooking time for more well done meat.

Makes 6 servings.

oriental grilled steak

Searing steaks or chops over a high flame gives them a crispy outside crust that seals in tenderness and precious juices.

⅓ cup	soy sauce
2 tablespoons	brown sugar
2 tablespoons	lemon juice
2 tablespoons	vegetable oil
⅓ cup	minced green onion
1	garlic clove, minced
¼ teaspoon	grated fresh ginger root
1	beef sirloin steak, cut 1½ inches thick (about 2 lbs.)

In a bowl, stir together soy, sugar, lemon juice, oil, green onion, garlic and ginger. Pour into large plastic bag. Place steak in bag with marinade and seal well. Turn so that meat is well coated with marinade. Refrigerate for 3-4 hours. Remove meat from marinade and place on grill over medium to high heat. Cook for 6-8 minutes per side, basting periodically with marinade.

Makes 6 servings.

zucchini-stuffed flank steak

When serving, carve meat into relatively thin slices for easy eating.

3 tablespoons	chopped onion
½ cup	chopped fresh mushrooms
1	small zucchini, chopped
2 tablespoons	butter or margerine
½ cup	fine, dry bread crumbs
1 teaspoon	dried leaf oregano
1 teaspoon	dried leaf basil
¾ teaspoon	salt
¼ teaspoon	ground pepper
1	flank steak (about 1¾ lbs.)
2 tablespoons	vegetable oil
1	garlic clove, minced
1 tablespoon	chopped parsley

In a fry pan, cook onion, mushroom and zucchini in butter over moderate heat until tender; remove from heat and stir in bread crumbs, oregano, basil, salt and pepper. Spoon filling mixture onto flank steak and roll up as a jelly roll. Tie securely with string. In a small bowl, stir together oil, garlic and parsley. Place stuffed steak on grill over low heat. Baste with seasoned oil. Cover grill and continue cooking for about 45 minutes, turning and basting every 10 minutes. Carve.

Makes 4-6 servings.

delicious main dishes

wined steak

Though the recipe calls for red wine, you may use white wine or dry vermouth.

1 cup	red wine
2 tablespoons	vegetable oil
1	garlic clove, minced
¼ teaspoon	dried leaf thyme
¼ teaspoon	ground pepper
¼ teaspoon	salt
1	porterhouse, sirloin or T-bone steak (about 2 lbs.), cut ¾-inch thick

In a bowl, stir together wine, oil, garlic, thyme, pepper and salt. Pour into large plastic bag. Place steak in bag with marinade; seal bag. Allow to marinate, refrigerated, for 24 hours, turning 3 times. Remove meat from marinade and cook on grill over high heat until meat reaches desired degree of doneness. For rare steak, cook for about 5-7 minutes per side.

Makes 4-6 servings.

round steak italienne

If you're short of time for marinating this recipe, leave the meat at room temperature in the marinade for 2 hours only.

1 envelope (6 oz.)	Italian salad dressing mix
⅓ cup	vegetable oil
3 tablespoons	wine vinegar
2 tablespoons	lemon juice
1½ lbs.	round steak, cut 1½-inches thick
2	medium tomatoes, cut into wedges

In a bowl, stir together salad dressing mix, oil, vinegar and lemon juice. Pour into large plastic bag. Cut meat into strips ¼-inch thick or less and place in bag with marinade. Tie bag securely. Turn so that meat is well coated with marinade. Refrigerate for 4-6 hours. Thread meat and tomatoes alternately on skewers. Place skewers on grill. Baste with marinade and cook over high heat for about 5 minutes. Baste again and turn meat, cooking for another 5 minutes.

Makes 6 servings

pepper steaks

For a spicier flavor, use hot as well as sweet bell peppers.

3	green peppers, seeded and sliced
1 teaspoon	salt
½ teaspoon	ground pepper
½ teaspoon	Worcestershire sauce
2 tablespoons	butter or margarine
6	cube steaks
	aluminum foil

Make pouch with double thickness of aluminum foil. Place peppers in pouch. Sprinkle with salt, pepper and Worcestershire sauce; dot with butter. Seal foil well and place pouch in covered grill over low heat. Cook for about 15 minutes, then turn grill up to medium-high and cook cube steaks to desired doneness. To serve, spoon peppers over cube steaks.

Makes 6 servings.

onion-crusted steaks

Canned french fried onions give steaks a crisp and not overpowering onion flavor.

4	rib-eye beef steaks, cut about ½-inch thick
2 tablespoons	vegetable oil
1 can (3 oz.)	french fried onions
1 teaspoon	salt
1 teaspoon	paprika

Brush steaks with oil and set aside. In cup of blender or food processor, crush onions to make crumbs. In a bowl, stir together crushed onion, salt and paprika. Dip steaks into crumb mixture and place on grill. Cook steaks over high heat to desired degree of doneness or about 5 minutes per side for medium.

Makes 4 servings.

marinated london broil

While many cuts of meat at the market may be called London Broil, select a flank steak. This cut grills quickly and will be tender if carved correctly.

1	flank steak (about 3 lbs.)
¾ cup	vegetable oil
⅓ cup	cider vinegar
6	scallions, minced
1 tablespoon	salt
1 teaspoon	ground pepper

Place flank steak in large plastic bag. In a bowl, stir together oil, vinegar, onion, salt and pepper. Pour into bag over meat. Tie bag securely and place in refrigerator. Marinate for 2-3 hours, turning bag frequently so meat will be well seasoned. Remove meat from bag and place on grill. Cook in covered grill for about 10-15 minutes, turning and basting occasionally. Carve diagonally, cutting across fibers of meat.

Makes 4-6 servings.

roast tenderloin of beef

Because tenderloin is so lean, it should be basted with oil before cooking and cooked at a high temperature for a short time to seal in juices.

1	4 lb. beef tenderloin
2 tablespoons	vegetable oil

Rub outside of tenderloin with oil and place on grill. Cook over high heat, turning periodically, for 10-12 minutes. Test for doneness with meat thermometer. (Internal temperature will be 130° F for rare; 140° F for medium). Allow meat to rest for 5 minutes before carving. Serve with Herbed Mustard Sauce.

Makes 6-8 servings.

peppered eye of the round roast

The flavor of this dish is rather like steak au poivre.

1 tablespoon	whole black peppercorns
1 tablespoon	whole white peppercorns
2 teaspoons	dried thyme leaves
1	3 lb. eye of the round roast, well-trimmed

In mortar and pestle, crush black and white peppercorns. In a shallow bowl, stir together crushed peppercorns with thyme. Roll roast in seasoning mixture, coating thoroughly. Wrap meat and refrigerate for 2 hours. Insert rotisserie rod lengthwise through center of roast. Balance roast and tighten spit forks to fasten meat securely so that it turns only with the rod. Place rod on grill and cook meat over low heat in covered grill for about 45 minutes for medium rare meat. Adjust cooking time accordingly for desired degree of doneness. Remove meat from rod and allow to stand for 10 minutes before carving.

Makes 8-10 servings.

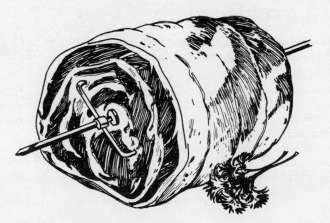

herbed mustard sauce

This hollandaise-like sauce, easily made in the blender or food processor, is excellent with roasted beef or lamb.

3	large egg yolks
4 teaspoons	lemon juice
1 tablespoon	Dijon mustard
½ teaspoon	salt
1 cup	unsalted butter, melted
2 teaspoons	chopped chives
2 teaspoons	chopped parsley
½ teaspoon	dried leaf tarragon

In cup of blender or food processor, beat together egg yolks, lemon juice, mustard and salt. While machine is running, very slowly beat in butter by pouring into eggs in a thin stream. Spoon sauce into bowl and stir in chives, parsley and tarragon.

Makes about 1½ cups.

rotisserie rib of beef

Nothing is more elegant than a beef rib roast browned to perfection. To make sure that the meat is done just the way you like it, use a meat thermometer.

1	4 lb. rib eye of beef roast

Insert rotisserie rod lengthwise through center of roast. Adjust holding forks and test balance; readjust as necessary. Place roast on grill; place drip pan directly under meat. Turn on spit and cook roast over low heat in covered grill for about 35 minutes and test for doneness with meat thermometer. Thermometer will register 140° F. for rare; 160° F. for medium and 170° F. for well-done. Adjust cooking time to match desired doneness. Allow meat to rest for at least 10 minutes before carving.

Makes about 10 servings.

barbecued brisket of beef

A flavorful way to keep you out of the hot kitchen during the summer.

1	brisket of beef (about 3½ lbs.)
1 can (10½ oz.)	condensed onion soup
1 can (8 oz.)	tomato sauce
3 tablespoons	honey
¼ cup	cider vinegar
1 tablespoon	lemon juice
1	garlic clove, minced
2 teaspoons	Worcestershire sauce
½ teaspoon	salt
⅛ teaspoon	crushed red pepper
	aluminum foil

Place brisket in 9 x 13-inch metal baking pan. In a bowl, stir together soup, tomato sauce, honey, vinegar, lemon juice, garlic, Worcestershire sauce, salt and pepper; pour over meat. Cover pan tightly with foil. Place pan on grill rack over moderately high heat. Cook, covered, for 15 minutes. Lower heat to low and continue cooking for 2 hours or until brisket is tender. To serve, carve meat across grain. Spoon sauce over meat.

Makes 12 servings.

tomatoey short ribs

Select short ribs that are meaty and well trimmed.

1	Bermuda onion, sliced
¼ cup	vegetable oil, divided
4	short ribs of beef (about 2½ lbs.)
1 bottle (12 oz.)	beer
2 tablespoons	tomato paste
½ teaspoon	salt
½ teaspoon	dried leaf thyme
½ teaspoon	ground pepper
2	bay leaves

In Dutch oven over moderate heat, cook onion in 2 tablespoons oil until tender, not browned; remove onions from pan and set aside. Add remaining oil and short ribs. Cook until meat is browned on all sides. Add beer, tomato paste, salt, thyme, pepper and bay leaves. Cover and simmer for about 1¼ hours or until meat is tender. Remove short ribs from sauce and set aside. Continue to cook liquid, uncovered for about 25 minutes. Place short ribs on grill over low to moderate heat; baste with cooking liquid. Cover grill and continue to cook ribs, basting and turning periodically for about 15-20 minutes.

Makes 4 servings.

cognac-marinated beef

Tarragon and cognac give these kebobs a distinctive flavor.

½ cup	water
¼ cup	cognac
2 tablespoons	vegetable oil
2 teaspoons	Worcestershire sauce
1 teaspoon	instant bouillon granules
1 teaspoon	dried leaf tarragon
1 teaspoon	prepared mustard
½ teaspoon	salt
2 lbs.	sirloin tips, cut into cubes
	metal or wooden skewers

In a bowl, stir together water, cognac, oil, Worcestershire sauce, bouillion, tarragon, mustard and salt. Pour mixture into large plastic bag. Place meat in bag and seal well. Turn bag so that meat is well coated with marinade. Refrigerate for at least 6 hours. Remove meat from marinade and thread onto skewers. Place on grill over medium to high heat and cook, covered, until meat reaches desired degree of doneness (about 10 minutes for rare meat). Turn periodically during cooking.

Makes 4-6 servings.

calves liver olé

A crispy, spicy, and oh so delicious way to prepare liver.

1 envelope (1¼ oz.)	taco seasoning mix
2 tablespoons	flour
3 tablespoons	butter or margarine, melted
1½ lbs.	calves liver

In a shallow bowl, stir together taco seasoning and flour. Pour butter into another shallow bowl. Dip liver first into butter and then into seasoning mix. Place liver on grill over medium heat. Cook in covered grill for 15 minutes. Turn twice and baste with remaining butter when turned.

Makes 4 servings.

pork and ham

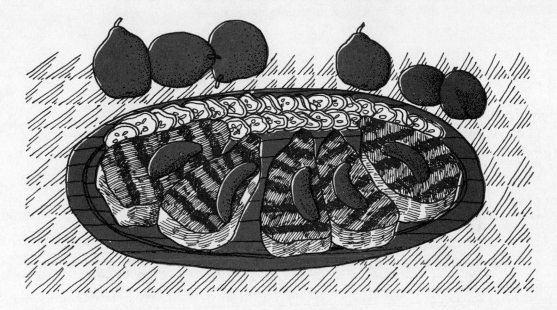

pork 'n' peaches

The Step-Up-Grid accessory for the grill keeps the pork roast far enough away from intense heat to allow slow roasting.

1	center cut pork roast (8 rib or 4-½ lb.)
3	medium peaches, cut into small pieces
1 tablespoon	seedless raisins
1 tablespoon	brown sugar
¼ teaspoon	grated lemon rind
1 cup	peach preserves
1 tablespoon	water

With a strong, sharp knife, make a pocket in the pork by cutting a deep slit down the length of the loin, going to within ½inch of the two ends and to within 1-inch of the other side. In a bowl, stir together peaches, raisins, brown sugar and lemon rind. Stuff pocket with peach mixture and tie or sew loin so that it will hold its shape during cooking. In a small bowl, stir together peach preserves and water. Place pork roast on Step-Up-Grid. Cook in covered grill over low heat for about 1 hour. Baste with peach preserves and continue cooking, basting every 5 minutes, for an additional 30 minutes. Roast is done when temperature reaches 170° F. on meat thermometer. Allow roast to stand for 10 minutes before carving.

Makes 6-8 servings.

delicious main dishes

pineapple-honey glazed ham

This ham is excellent hot from the grill wrapped for a picnic away from home or refrigerated and served cold.

1 cup	pineapple juice
½ cup	honey
4 tablespoons	soy sauce
1 teaspoon	grated fresh ginger root
1 teaspoon	dry mustard
1	fully cooked boneless ham (about 3 lb.)

In a bowl, stir together pineapple juice, honey, soy sauce, ginger and mustard. Place ham on grill over low heat and baste with sauce. Cover grill and cook for about 35 minutes, basting periodically. Turn ham once during cooking.

Makes about 6-8 servings.

apricot-glazed canadian bacon roast

Canadian-style bacon, which is cured and smoked pork loin, is usually lean. However, trim it carefully so there won't be any flare-ups from dripping fat.

1	Canadian-style bacon roast (about 3 lbs.)
1 jar (12 oz.)	apricot preserves
2 tablespoons	dry white wine

Insert spit rod horizontally through center of roast. Tighten spit forks at both ends and test for balance, readjusting if necessary. Place rod on grill; place drip pan on grill rack directly below roast. In a small saucepan, heat preserves with white wine. When preserves have melted, but are not too hot, pour into cup of blender or food processor and purée. Baste roast with preserves. Turn on spit and cover grill. Cook, basting periodically, over low heat for about 35 minutes or until meat thermometer registers 170°F.

Makes about 8-10 servings.

roast smoked pork loin

Because smoked pork has the richness of ham, you may want to serve smaller portions.

¼ cup	soy sauce
3 tablespoons	water
2 tablespoons	sweet vermouth
2 tablespoons	honey
1	garlic clove, minced
1	smoked pork loin roast (about 3 lbs.)

In a bowl, stir together soy sauce, water, vermouth, honey and garlic. Place pork loin on Step-Up-Grid of grill. Baste roast with soy sauce mixture and cook in covered grill over low heat for about 1¼ hours, basting periodically. Roast is done when temperature reaches 170° F.

Makes about 6 servings.

rotisserie rolled pork loin

Balancing the roast carefully on the rotisserie rod will save wear on the rotisserie motor. It will also keep meat from slipping and cooking unevenly.

1	rolled pork loin roast (4 lbs.)
1 jar (10 oz.)	currant jelly
2 tablespoons	orange juice
2 tablespoons	lemon juice
1 teaspoon	grated orange rind
1 teaspoon	grated lemon rind

Insert rotisserie rod horizontally through center of pork loin. Tighten spit forks at both ends and test for balance, readjusting if necessary. Place rod on grill; place drip pan on grill rack directly below roast. Turn on rotisserie and cook roast over low heat in covered grill for 1¼ hours. Meanwhile in a small saucepan over moderate heat, stir together jelly, orange juice, lemon juice, orange rind and lemon rind. Remove from heat when jelly is melted. Baste roast with glaze and continue cooking for an additional 30 minutes, basting periodically. Roast is done when thermometer registers 170°F. Allow roast to stand for 10 minutes before carving.

Makes about 10-12 servings.

sherried butterflied pork tenderloin

Simplify the preparation by asking your butcher to butterfly the pork tenderloin.

½ cup	medium dry sherry
⅓ cup	maple syrup
2 teaspoons	soy sauce
½ cup	chopped scallion
2 teaspoons	grated fresh ginger
2	garlic cloves, minced
3 (1½ lb., each)	pork tenderloins, butterflied

In a bowl, stir together sherry, maple syrup, soy, scallion, ginger and garlic. Pour into large plastic bag. Place meat in bag and seal well. Allow meat to marinate for 4-6 hours, turning periodically. Remove meat from marinade and place on grill over low heat. Cook in covered grill for about 25-30 minutes, basting periodically with marinade. To serve, carve crosswise into thin slices.

Makes 6-8 servings.

glazed ham steak

Grilled pineapple slices are an excellent accompaniment for the glazed ham.

½ cup	frozen concentrated orange juice, thawed
2 tablespoons	lemon juice
½ cup	dark corn syrup
1 tablespoon	vegetable oil
1	ham steak (about 1½ to 2 lbs.), cut 1-inch thick

In a bowl, stir together juice concentrate, lemon juice, corn syrup and oil. Slash fat edge of ham slice and place on grill. Brush with sauce. Grill over low to medium heat for 10-15 minutes in covered grill, turning and basting occasionally during cooking.

Makes 6 servings.

sweet tomato barbecued pork chops

Cooking chops — pork or lamb — is easier if a grill basket is used for quick turning.

1 cup	apricot preserves
¼ cup	prepared tomato sauce
⅓ cup	cider vinegar
¼ cup	medium dry sherry
2 tablespoons	soy sauce
2 tablespoons	brown sugar
2 tablespoons	vegetable oil
1 teaspoon	salt
4 to 6	pork chops, cut ¾ to 1-inch thick

In a saucepan over moderate heat, stir together preserves, tomato sauce, vinegar, sherry, soy, brown sugar, oil and salt. Simmer, covered, for 15 minutes. Place chops in grill basket and put basket on grill. Baste with sauce mixture. Cook over medium heat in covered grill for 30 minutes, turning and basting every 5 minutes during cooking.

Makes 4-6 servings.

orange bourbon pork chops

For quicker cooking, pork chops may be butterflied.

½ cup	orange marmalade
2 tablespoons	orange juice
2 tablespoons	bourbon
4 to 6	pork chops, cut ¾ to 1-inch thick

In a bowl, stir together marmalade, orange juice and bourbon. Place chops in grill basket and baste with marmalade mixture. Place basket on grill and cook over medium heat in covered grill for 30 minutes, turning and basting every 5 minutes during cooking.

Makes 4-6 servings.

PORK CHART

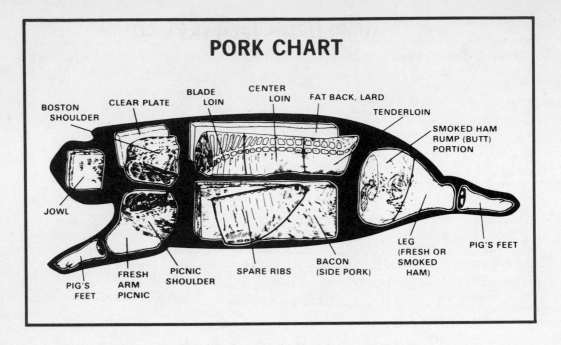

BOSTON SHOULDER

CLEAR PLATE

BLADE LOIN

CENTER LOIN

FAT BACK, LARD

TENDERLOIN

SMOKED HAM RUMP (BUTT) PORTION

JOWL

PIG'S FEET

FRESH ARM PICNIC

PICNIC SHOULDER

SPARE RIBS

BACON (SIDE PORK)

LEG (FRESH OR SMOKED HAM)

PIG'S FEET

pear and almond stuffed pork chops

Use firm pears for this recipe.

6	loin pork chops, about 1½-inches thick
4 tablespoons	butter or margarine
½ cup	celery
2	small pears, cored and chopped
1 cup	fine, dry bread crumbs
2 tablespoons	chopped almonds
½ teaspoon	salt
⅛ teaspoon	ground pepper

Make a slit in each chop by cutting from fat side almost to bone; set aside. In a fry pan, melt butter over moderate heat. Add celery and pears, cooking until celery is tender. Remove from heat and stir in bread crumbs, almonds, salt and pepper. Spoon stuffing into each chop and securely fasten pocket opening with food picks. Grill chops over low heat for about 20 minutes per side. Remove picks before serving.

Makes 6 servings.

pork chops teriyaki

The easiest way to peel garlic for this or any recipe is to place it on a cutting board, place the flat side of a French knife over the garlic cloves and hit the side of the knife facing you, being careful not to touch the blade. Peel can easily be removed from crushed garlic cloves.

1 can (10½ oz.)	condensed beef broth
1 can (8 oz.)	tomato sauce
3	garlic cloves, minced
¼ cup	honey
¼ cup	soy sauce
1 teaspoon	dry mustard
¼ teaspoon	grated fresh ginger root
8	loin pork chops, about 1½-inches thick

In a bowl, stir together broth, tomato sauce, garlic, honey, soy sauce, mustard and ginger root. Place pork chops in large plastic bag. Pour teriyaki marinade over chops and seal bag well. Turn bag so meat is well covered with marinade. Refrigerate for 3-5 hours. Remove chops from marinade and place on grill. Cook in covered grill for about 20 minutes, basting periodically with marinade.

Makes 8 servings.

honey curried pork chops

These pork chops are butterflied for quicker cooking. Either butterfly them yourself or ask the butcher for help.

⅓ cup	honey
¼ cup	butter or margarine, melted
1 teaspoon	dry mustard
¾ teaspoon	curry powder
4	loin pork chops, cut 2-inches thick and butterflied

In a bowl, stir together honey, butter, mustard and curry powder. Place chops on grill over medium heat. Baste with flavored butter. Cook in covered grill for about 15-20 minutes, turning and basting every 5 minutes.

Makes 4 servings.

chinese-style barbecued spareribs

Hoisin sauce is available in Chinese grocery stores or specialty sections of the supermarket.

½ cup	medium dry sherry
½ cup	hoisin sauce
¼ cup	soy sauce
4	garlic cloves, minced
½ teaspoon	grated fresh ginger
2 tablespoons	sugar
4 lbs.	pork spareribs

In a bowl, stir together sherry, hoisin sauce, soy sauce, garlic, ginger and sugar. Pour into large plastic bag. Place spareribs in bag and close bag securely. Turn bag over several times so that marinade coats meat. Place ribs in refrigerator and allow to marinate for 3-4 hours, turning periodically.

To cook, remove spareribs from marinade and place on grill over low heat. Cook in covered grill for about 15 minutes per side. Cut meat into individual ribs to serve.

Makes 4 servings.

old-fashioned barbecued spareribs

This recipe makes enough sauce for two cookouts, so the extra sauce may be frozen for another day.

1 bottle (14 oz.)	catsup
½ cup	water
6 tablespoons	brown sugar
¼ cup	cider vinegar
3 tablespoons	Worcestershire sauce
2 tablespoons	lemon juice
1	onion, grated
1 teaspoon	ground mustard
¼ teaspoon	salt
4 lbs.	pork spareribs

In a large saucepan, stir together catsup, water, brown sugar, vinegar, Worcestershire sauce, lemon juice, onion, mustard and salt. Cook over moderate heat for about 45 minutes.

Place spareribs on grill over low heat. Baste with barbecue sauce. Cover grill and continue cooking for 45 minutes, turning and basting every 10 minutes.

Makes 4 servings.

spareribs cacciatore

The prepared sauce makes this recipe simple and delicious.

1	medium onion, peeled and thinly sliced
1	green pepper, seeded and thinly sliced
1	garlic clove, minced
3 tablespoons	vegetable oil
1½ cups	thinly sliced fresh mushrooms
1 jar (15½ oz.)	Italian cooking sauce
4 lbs.	pork spareribs

In a fry pan over moderate heat, sauté onion, green pepper and garlic in vegetable oil. When tender, stir in mushrooms and continue cooking for 5 minutes; remove from heat and stir in ½ cooking sauce. Set aside. Place spareribs on grill over low heat in covered grill. Cook for 25 minutes, turning every 5 minutes. Baste ribs with plain cooking sauce and cook for an additional 20 minutes, turning occasionally. For the final basting, use sauce with vegetables.

Makes 4 servings.

spicy country-style ribs

This recipe is only for those who like hot flavors.

4 lbs.	pork country ribs, cut into serving pieces
½ cup	prepared hot taco sauce
1 tablespoon	lemon juice
1 can (3 oz.)	whole green chilies, drained, seeded and chopped
2 tablespoons	minced onion

In a large covered pot, cook ribs in boiling water to cover. Allow to simmer for 60 minutes or until tender. Drain well. Meanwhile, in a bowl, stir together taco sauce, lemon juice, chilies and onion. Place ribs in grill basket or on grill. Cook for 10 minutes over medium heat. Baste with sauce and continue cooking, turning and basting occasionally, for an additional 15-20 minutes.

Makes 4 servings.

pork sate

Lime and ginger give this Southeast Asian dish its special character.

¼ cup	fresh lime juice
2 tablespoons	soy sauce
2 tablespoons	water
1 piece (3-inches)	fresh hot chili
1	small onion, cut into chunks
2 teaspoons	grated fresh ginger root
2 teaspoons	salt
1½ lbs.	boneless pork, cut into 1-inch cubes wooden or metal skewers

In cup of blender or food processor, purée lime juice, soy sauce, water, chili, onion, ginger and salt. Pour into plastic bag. Add pork to liquid in bag and seal well. Turn bag so that meat is well coated with marinade. Refrigerate for 2-4 hours. Thread meat on skewers and place on grill. Cook over low heat in covered grill, basting periodically with marinade and turning, for about 25 minutes.

Makes 4-6 servings.

sweet and spicy ham kebobs

Ham kebobs are especially good when served with a fruited rice.

½ cup	sweet and spicy bottled salad dressing
¼ cup	minced green pepper
1 tablespoon	Worcestershire sauce
1½ lbs.	fully cooked boneless ham, cut into 1-inch pieces
1	Bermuda onion, cut into wedges
	fresh pineapple chunks
	wooden or metal skewers

In a bowl, stir together salad dressing, green peppers and Worcestershire sauce. Thread ham, onion wedges and pineapple onto skewers. Place on grill and baste with dressing. Cook over low heat, turning and basting often, for 15-20 minutes.

Makes 4-6 servings.

pork kebobs with beer glaze

Be sure pork is lean and well-trimmed to prevent flare-ups during cooking.

½ cup	catsup
½ cup	cider vinegar
½ cup	beer
1 tablespoon	soy sauce
2 teaspoons	Worcestershire sauce
¼ teaspoon	ground pepper
1½ lbs.	boneless pork, cut into 1-inch cubes
2	medium green peppers, seeded and cut into chunks
	metal or wooden skewers

In a small saucepan, stir together catsup, vinegar, beer, soy, Worcestershire sauce and pepper. Over moderate heat bring liquid to simmer and cook for 15 minutes. Thread pork and green peppers alternately on skewers and place on grill. Baste with beer glaze, cover grill and cook over low heat for 20-25 minutes. Turn and baste every 5 minutes.

Makes 6 servings.

pork kebobs with acorn squash

Grapefruit juice baste has a tart sweetness which is perfect with the squash and pork.

1	small acorn squash, seeded and cut into twelfths
1½ lbs.	boneless pork
1 can (6 oz.)	concentrated grapefruit juice
¼ cup	orange marmalade
2 teaspoons	soy sauce

In a saucepan over moderate heat, cook squash in salted boiling water until just barely tender; cool immediately. Thread squash and pork alternately on skewers. Place skewers on grill. In a bowl, stir together juice concentrate, marmalade and soy sauce; baste kebobs with sauce. Cook over low heat in covered grill for about 25 minutes, turning and basting occasionally.

Makes 6 servings.

kielbasa kebobs

Since kielbasa is generally fully cooked when purchased, the cooking time is very short.

1 lb.	kielbasa, cut into 1½-inch thick pieces
12	small whole onions, peeled and parboiled
12	large button mushrooms
1	red bellpepper, seeded and cut into chunks
	metal or wooden skewers

Alternate kielbasa, onion, mushroom and pepper on skewers. Place on grill over low to medium heat and cook, covered for 5-10 minutes. Turn and continue cooking for an additional 5-10 minutes or until meat and vegetables are browned.

Makes 4 servings.

chili-brushed knockwurst

An easy-to-make baste that is also delicious on frankfurters or hamburgers.

½cup	prepared chili sauce
2 tablespoons	Worcestershire sauce
2 tablespoons	vegetable oil
2 tablespoons	minced onion
4 teaspoons	molasses
6	knockwurst

In a bowl, stir together chili sauce, Worcestershire sauce, oil, onion and molasses. Score knockwurst on the the bias and place on grill over medium to high heat. Baste with chili sauce mixture. Turn and baste periodically, cooking for about 10 minutes.

Makes 6 servings.

snappy-grilled bratwurst

These milk pork and veal sausages are delicious with the mustard-scallion baste.

4	bratwurst
¼ cup	prepared mustard
¼ cup	chopped scallion
2 tablespoons	cider vinegar
1 tablespoon	vegetable oil
1 teaspoon	prepared horseradish

Split bratwurst horizontally almost in half. Place cut-side-down on grill. In a bowl, stir together mustard, scallion, vinegar, oil and horseradish. Baste bratwurst with mustard. Cook in covered grill over medium heat for 10 minutes, basting periodically with sauce.

Makes 4 servings.

frank and bean bundles

Also great for family camping trips. Can be prepared ahead and transported.

4	frankfurters, sliced into 2-inch chunks
1 can (28 oz.)	brick oven baked beans
¼ cup	chopped onion
¼ cup	chopped green pepper
	aluminum foil

Make 4 aluminum foil pouches. Fill each first with franks, then baked beans, onion and green pepper. Wrap foil around contents and seal well. Place pouches on grill over low heat and cook, covered, for 20 minutes. Stir and serve.

Makes 4 servings.

franks 'n' swiss cheese

To make this a kid's favorite, change the cheese to American.

8	frankfurters
8 pieces	Swiss cheese, cut into julienne shape to fit frankfurters
8	bacon strips
	food picks

Cut franks almost through horizontally. Place piece of cheese between frankfurter halves. Close frankfurters and wrap with bacon strip; secure with food picks. Place franks on grill over medium heat and cook, covered, for 10 minutes, turning periodically.

Makes 8 servings.

delicious main dishes

sausages with peppers and onions

Green peppers make a handy cooking container for the onions.

4	green peppers, seeded
½ teaspoon	salt
½ teaspoon	dried leaf oregano
¼ teaspoon	ground pepper
1	Bermuda onion, peeled and cut into wedges
1½ lbs.	sweet Italian sausages (about 8 links)

Sprinkle insides of peppers with salt, oregano and pepper. Fill peppers with onion wedges and place on grill. Cover grill and cook over low heat for about 15 minutes or until peppers are lightly browned on outsides, turning periodically. Place sausages on grill and continue cooking for about 20 minutes, turning sausages and peppers during cooking.

Makes 4 servings.

poultry

parmesan chicken

A coating of sesame seeds and Parmesan cheese gives this chicken a crispy texture.

2	eggs
6 tablespoons	sesame seeds
¼ cup	grated Parmesan cheese
¼ cup	flour
1½ teaspoons	salt
¼ teaspoon	ground pepper
1	broiler-fryer chicken

In a shallow bowl, beat together eggs with 1 tablespoon water; set aside. In another bowl, stir together sesame seeds and cheese. In a third bowl, stir together flour, salt and pepper. Dip whole chicken first into flour mixture, then into the egg mixture and last into the sesame seed-cheese mixture. Be sure that chicken is well coated with each dipping.

Insert spit rod through center of chicken. Adjust holding forks; truss chicken; test balance. Place drip pan on rack below cooking grill. Put spit rod in place on grill, being sure that drip pan is directly under chicken. Turn on motor. Grill chicken over low heat in covered grill for about 1 hour.

Makes 4 servings.

delicious main dishes

orange-cranberry chicken

Here's chicken with a rosy color and tart sweetness.

1 can (8 oz.)	whole berry cranberry sauce
1 teaspoon	grated orange rind
⅔ cup	orange juice
1	whole broiler-fryer chicken

In cup of blender or food processor, purée cranberry sauce with orange rind and orange juice. Truss chicken; insert spit rod through center of chicken. Adjust holding forks; test balance. Put spit rod in place on grill; place drip pan on rack directly under chicken. Baste chicken with cranberry mixture. Turn on motor. Grill chicken over low heat in covered grill, basting periodically, for about 1 hour.

Makes 4 servings.

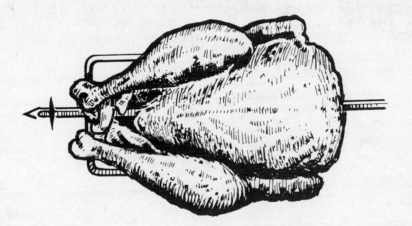

chicken with pesto sauce

When fresh basil is not available, substitute Italian parsley or spinach leaves with 1 tablespoon dried basil leaves.

1	broiler-fryer chicken, cut into parts
½ teaspoon	salt
¼ teaspoon	ground pepper
1 teaspoon	dried basil leaves
¼ cup	vegetable oil
2	garlic cloves, minced
¼ cup	pine nuts or slivered almonds
1 bunch	fresh basil leaves (makes about 1½ cups)
¼ cup	grated Parmesan cheese

Sprinkle chicken with salt, pepper and dried basil. Place on grill and cook over low heat for 35-40 minutes in covered grill, turning periodically. Meanwhile, place oil, garlic, nuts, fresh basil and cheese in cup of blender or food processor and purée to make pesto sauce. To serve, spoon pesto sauce over cooked chicken.

Makes 4 servings.

chicken hoisin

Hoisin sauce gives the chicken a sweet richness.

¼ cup	hoisin sauce*
2 tablespoons	medium dry sherry
2 tablespoons	chicken broth
¼ cup	chopped scallion
2 tablespoons	soy sauce
1	broiler-fryer chicken, cut into parts

In a bowl, stir together hoisin sauce, sherry, broth, scallion and soy sauce. Place chicken on grill over low heat and baste with sauce mixture. Cook for about 35-40 minutes in covered grill, turning and basting frequently during cooking.

Makes 4 servings.

*Hoisin sauce is available in Chinese grocery stores.

chipper chicken

Vary the flavor by using a seasoned potato chip.

1 cup	potato chip crumbs
2 tablespoons	minced onion
½ teaspoon	paprika
⅓ cup	butter or margarine, melted
1	broiler-fryer chicken, cut into parts

In a bowl, stir together potato chip crumbs, onion and paprika. Pour butter into a shallow bowl. Dip chicken parts first into butter to coat and then into chip mixture. Place chicken parts on grill and cook over low heat for 35-40 minutes covered.

Makes 4 servings.

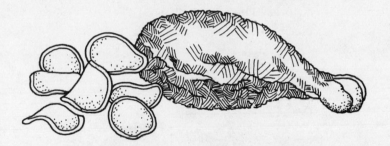

tandoori chicken

An Indian recipe for outdoor cooking.

1 cup	plain yogurt
¼ cup	lemon juice
2	garlic cloves, minced
½ teaspoon	salt
½ teaspoon	ground coriander
¼ teaspoon	grated fresh ginger root
¼ teaspoon	crushed fennel seeds
pinch	saffron
pinch	crushed red pepper
3 drops	red food coloring
1	broiler-fryer chicken, cut into parts

In a bowl, stir together yogurt, lemon juice, garlic, salt, coriander, ginger, fennel, saffron, pepper and food coloring. Place chicken in glass pan or bowl and spoon yogurt mixture over chicken, coating all pieces well. Cover and refrigerate for 4-6 hours. Remove chicken from marinade and place on grill rack. Cook, covered, over low heat for about 45 minutes, turning and basting periodically with marinade.

Makes 4 servings.

delicious main dishes

lime-grilled chicken

Plan to buy at least 3 limes to make ¼ cup lime juice.

¼ cup	fresh lime juice
2 tablespoons	vegetable oil
2 tablespoons	minced onion
½ teaspoon	grated lime rind
½ teaspoon	salt
¼ teaspoon	ground pepper
1	broiler-fryer chicken, cut into parts

In a bowl, stir together lime juice, vegetable oil, onion, lime rind, salt and pepper. Place chicken parts on grill over low heat and baste with lime juice mixture. Cook in covered grill, basting and turning periodically, for about 45 minutes.

Makes 4 servings.

blue cheese-basted chicken

This is chicken with a zing for those real lovers of blue cheese.

1 cup (4 oz.)	crumbled Danish blue cheese
3 tablespoons	milk or cream
2 tablespoons	vegetable oil
1 tablespoon	Worcestershire sauce
3 tablespoons	minced onion
½ teaspoon	salt
¼ teaspoon	ground pepper
1	broiler-fryer chicken, cut into parts

In a bowl, beat together cheese, milk, oil, Worcestershire sauce, onion, salt and pepper. Place chicken on grill and baste with blue cheese sauce. Cover grill and cook over low heat for about 35 minutes, turning and basting periodically with sauce.

Makes 4 servings.

chicken italian

Using a prepared sauce mix makes this recipe particularly easy.

1¼ cups	buttermilk biscuit mix
1 package (1½ oz.)	spaghetti sauce mix
2	broiler-fryer chickens, cut into parts

In a bowl, stir together biscuit mix and sauce mix. Dip chicken parts into dry ingredients so that all pieces are well coated. Place chicken parts on grill rack over low heat. Cook in covered grill, turning occasionally, for about 30-35 minutes.

Makes 8 servings.

sweet relish-tomato sauced chicken

For this recipe, select any chicken parts that you prefer or that are on sale at the market. The flavor is yummy sweet whether you use thighs, quarters, wings or legs.

⅔ cup	catsup
2 tablespoons	sweet pickle relish
1 tablespoon	minced onion
1 tablespoon	vegetable oil
1 teaspoon	Worcestershire sauce
1	broiler-fryer chicken, cut into parts

In a bowl, stir together catsup, relish, onion, vegetable oil and Worcestershire sauce. Place chicken on grill and baste with sauce. Cook over low heat for 30-35 minutes in covered grill, turning and basting occasionally.

Makes 4 servings.

chicken thighs with feta cheese

Chicken thighs are easily boned with a sharp knife.

1 cup	plain yogurt
2 tablespoons	prepared Dijon mustard
1 teaspoon	Worcestershire sauce
¼ teaspoon	salt
3 tablespoons	fresh chopped mint, divided
8	boned chicken thighs
½ cup	crumbled feta cheese

In a bowl, stir together, yogurt, mustard, Worcestershire sauce, salt and 1½ tablespoons mint; set aside. Wrap each chicken thigh around 1 tablespoon feta cheese. Tie or secure with food picks. Place chicken thighs in shallow container. Spoon yogurt mixture over chicken and allow to marinate for 1 hour. Remove from marinade and cook on grill rack over low heat in covered grill for 35 minutes. Turn and baste periodically with marinade.

Makes 4 servings.

honey-mint chicken thighs

If possible, substitute fresh mint for dried mint for a fuller flavor.

½ cup	honey
¼ cup	vegetable oil
2 tablespoons	dried mint leaves, crushed
½ teaspoon	salt
8	chicken thighs (about 2 lbs.)

In a bowl, stir together honey, oil, mint leaves and salt. Place chicken thighs on grill over low heat. Cover grill and cook chicken for 15 minutes, turning once. Baste with honey mixture and cook for an additional 20 minutes, turning and basting periodically.

Makes 4-8 servings.

herb-coated chicken wings

Use either plain or cornbread stuffing.

1½ cups	herb seasoned stuffing mix
¼ teaspoon	ground sage
¼ teaspoon	salt
¼ cup	butter or margarine, melted
2 lbs.	chicken wings

Place stuffing mix in cup of blender or food processor and grind into crumbs; pour into shallow bowl. Add sage and salt; stir to mix well. Pour butter into another bowl. Dip chicken wings first into butter and then into seasoning mix. Place chicken wings on grill over low heat. Cook in covered grill for 30 minutes, turning periodically during cooking.

Makes 4 servings.

crunchy-stuffed chicken breasts

For extra nutty flavor, toast walnuts before chopping for stuffing.

½ cup	water
½ cup	butter or margarine, divided
1½ cups	herb seasoned stuffing
⅓ cup	chopped walnuts
¼ cup	chopped celery
2	whole chicken breasts
½ teaspoon	salt
¼ teaspoon	ground pepper

In a small saucepan, bring water and 2½ tablespoons butter to boil. Place stuffing in bowl; pour water-butter over stuffing and stir until well mixed. Add nuts and celery to stuffing and stir again. Sprinkle insides of chicken breasts with salt and pepper. Spoon stuffing into breasts. Tie breasts well with string to hold in filling. Place chicken on grill; cook, covered, over low heat for 1½ hours, basting periodically with remaining butter.

Makes 4 servings.

scallion-pepper chicken rolls

A quick and delicious recipe for boneless chicken breast filling.

2	whole chicken breasts, halved and boned
¾ teaspoon	salt, divided
¼ teaspoon	ground pepper, divided
4	scallions, cut to width of chicken breasts
1	medium green pepper, seeded and cut into eighths lengthwise
3 tablespoons	vegetable oil
2 tablespoons	red wine vinegar
¼ teaspoon	dried marjoram leaves
¼ teaspoon	Summer Savory

Pound chicken breasts to flatten. Sprinkle insides of breasts with ½ teaspoon salt and ⅛ teaspoon pepper. Place a scallion and 2 pieces of green pepper at one end of each chicken breast and roll up breasts. Secure with string or small skewers. In a bowl, stir together oil, vinegar, marjoram leaves, Summer Savory and remaining salt and pepper. Place chicken rolls on grill and baste with seasoned oil. Cook in covered grill for 20 minutes, turning and basting periodically.

Makes 4 servings.

chicken roll-ups with cheddar and bacon

Using canned crumbled bacon makes this recipe preparation just one step quicker.

½ cup	finely shredded cheddar cheese, divided
¼ cup	crumbled bacon
3 tablespoons	fine, dry bread crumbs
2	whole chicken breasts, halved and boned
3 tablespoons	butter or margarine, melted

In a bowl, stir together ¼ cup cheese with bacon. In another bowl, stir together remaining cheese with bread crumbs. Flatten chicken breasts. Place ¼ cheese-bacon mixture at one end of each chicken breast. Roll up breasts and secure with string or small skewer. Pour butter into shallow dish. Dip chicken breasts into butter and then into cheese-crumb mixture. Place breasts on grill over low heat. Cook in covered grill for about 20 minutes, turning several times during cooking.

Makes 4 servings.

chicken kebobs hawaiian

Fresh pineapple makes this outdoor recipe especially good.

1 can (6 oz.)	concentrated frozen pineapple juice
4 teaspoons	soy sauce
½ teaspoon	grated fresh ginger
2	green peppers, seeded and cut in eighths
½	fresh pineapple
3	whole chicken breasts
	metal or wooden skewers

In a small bowl, stir together pineapple juice, soy sauce and ginger; set aside. Remove rind from pineapple and cut pineapple into chunks. Cut chicken breasts into strips or chunks. Thread peppers, pineapple and chicken on skewers. Place on grill over low heat and baste with pineapple juice mixture. Cook in covered grill for about 25 minutes, turning and basting periodically during cooking.

Makes 4-6 servings.

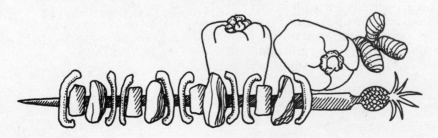

chicken yakitori

Chicken and scallion kebobs with a Japanese flair.

½ cup	sake or dry sherry
½ cup	chicken broth
½ cup	soy sauce
1 tablespoon	brown sugar
½ teaspoon	grated fresh ginger root
2	whole chicken breasts, boned, skinned and cut into 1-inch pieces
8	scallions, cut into 1-inch lengths
	metal or wooden skewers

In a bowl, stir together sake, broth, soy, sugar and ginger. Thread chicken and scallions on skewers. Dip skewers into sauce and place on grill over high heat. Baste frequently and cook for about 5 minutes on each side.

Makes 4 servings.

chicken livers with apple

Enjoy this combination as an entrée or hors d'oeuvre.

2	medium apples, cored and cut into thick wedges
1 lb.	chicken livers, trimmed
⅓ cup	vegetable oil
½ teaspoon	curry powder
½ teaspoon	ground ginger
½ teaspoon	salt
¼ teaspoon	ground pepper
	wooden or metal skewers

Alternate pieces of apple and chicken liver on skewers. In a small bowl, stir together oil, curry powder, ginger, salt and pepper. Baste apple and liver with seasoned oil and place on grill over medium heat. Cook in covered grill for about 15-20 minutes, basting and turning periodically.

Makes 4 servings as an entrée or 8 servings as an hors d'oeuvre.

game hens with kasha stuffing

Plan to serve either a half or whole game hen based on the size of the birds.

2 tablespoons	butter or margarine
1 cup	chopped scallion
15	medium fresh mushrooms, cleaned and quartered
1	egg, beaten
¾ cup	kasha or roasted buckwheat groats
1½ cups	chicken broth
¼ teaspoon	salt
¼ teaspoon	ground pepper
4	Cornish game hens, rinsed and drained
⅓ cup	dry vermouth
2 tablespoons	lemon juice
2 tablespoons	soy sauce
2 tablespoons	vegetable oil

In a fry pan over moderate heat, melt butter. Add scallion and mushrooms; sautée until scallion is tender and mushrooms cooked; remove from heat. In a bowl, stir together egg and kasha. Spoon kasha into fry pan and return to heat. Cook and stir until kasha grains are dry and separated. Pour broth over kasha and add salt and pepper. Cover fry pan and cook kasha for about 15-20 minutes. Remove from heat and cool. Stuff game hens with kasha and tie legs together. Insert rotisserie rod under legs and through centers of birds. Tighten spit forks at both ends of rod and test for balance, readjusting if necessary. Place rod on grill; place drip pan on grill directly below game hens. In a bowl, stir together vermouth, lemon juice, soy and vegetable oil. Baste birds with vermouth mixture and turn on rotisserie. Cook in covered grill for 45 minutes to 1 hour, basting periodically.

Makes 4 or 8 servings.

delicious main dishes

rotisserie duck with lemon

Oven pre-roasting allows fat to cook off before grilling.

1	duck (about 5 lbs.)
1 can (6 oz.)	frozen concentrated lemonade, defrosted
½	fresh lemon
1 tablespoon	cider vinegar

Pierce skin of duck in several places and place bird on rack of roasting pan. Cook in oven at 400°F. for one hour. Meanwhile, in a bowl, stir together lemonade, slivered rind from lemon and vinegar. Remove duck from oven and insert rotisserie rod under legs and through center of bird. Tie legs together and tie wings to chest. Tighten spit forks at both ends of rod and test for balance, readjusting if necessary. Place rod on grill; place drip pan on grill directly below duck. Baste duck with lemonade mixture and turn on spit. Cook in covered grill for about 30 minutes, basting periodically.

Makes 4 servings.

smoked duck

The duck has a robust flavor from the combination of hickory smoking and use of sesame oil in the basting sauce.

1	duck (about 5 lbs.)
¼ cup	white cider vinegar
¼ cup	sugar
2 tablespoons	medium dry sherry
2 tablespoons	chicken broth
½ teaspoon	soy sauce
⅛ teaspoon	grated fresh ginger root
4 drops	sesame oil

Soak 3-4 hickory chunks in water for 1 hour or more. Wrap in foil and puncture foil in several places to allow smoke to escape. Pierce skin of duck in several places and put bird on rack of roasting pan. Cook in 400° F.oven for 1 hour. Remove duck from oven and quarter. In a bowl, stir together vinegar, sugar, sherry, chicken broth, soy sauce, ginger and sesame oil. Place foil-wrapped chunks onto fire grate; turn grill on high for 15 minutes before cooking or until chunks smolder. Place duck quarters on grill and turn flame down to low. Baste with sauce. Cover grill and cook, basting and turning periodically, for 20-25 minutes.

Makes 4 servings.

outdoor grilled turkey

If you want stuffing for the turkey, prepare it separately. Do not stuff the bird.

1	turkey (6 to 8 lbs.)
¼ cup	vegetable oil
1 teaspoon	salt
1 teaspoon	rosemary leaves
¼ teaspoon	ground pepper

Remove giblets and rinse turkey. Tie legs together and secure wings to body. Insert rotisserie rod under legs and through center of the bird. Tighten spit forks at both ends and test for balance, readjusting if necessary. Place rod on grill; place drip pan on grill directly below turkey. In a bowl, stir together oil, salt, rosemary and pepper. Baste turkey with seasoned oil. Turn on rotisserie and cook turkey in covered grill for about 2 hours over low heat, basting periodically. Turkey is done when internal temperature reaches 180° F. Allow turkey to rest for 10 minutes before carving.

Makes about 8 servings.

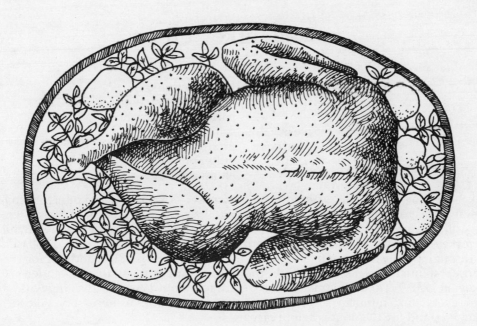

golden brown turkey thighs

When turkey parts are available at the market, they are usually a good buy.

1 cup	packed brown sugar
½ cup	vegetable oil
½ cup	catsup
½ cup	cider vinegar
⅓ cup	pineapple juice
⅓ cup	finely chopped onion
¼ cup	soy sauce
4	turkey thighs

In a bowl, stir together brown sugar, oil, catsup, vinegar, pineapple juice, onion and soy. Pour sauce into large plastic bag. Place turkey thighs in bag and seal well. Rotate bag to coat meat well with marinade. Allow to marinate for 2-3 hours at room temperature or overnight in refrigerator. Remove thighs from marinade and place on grill over low heat. Cook in covered grill for about 1 hour, basting periodically with marinade and turning. Halve turkey thighs to serve.

Makes 8 servings.

smoked turkey breast

Hickory chunks give the turkey a subtly smoked flavor.

3-4	hickory chunks
1	turkey breast (about 4 lbs.)
2	garlic cloves, crushed
1 teaspoon	salt
1 teaspoon	ground pepper
1 stick (¼ lb.)	butter or margarine, melted
	aluminum foil

Soak 3-4 hickory chunks in water for 1 hour or more. Wrap in foil and puncture foil in several places to allow smoke to escape. Place foil wrapped chunks onto fire grate; turn grill on high for 15 minutes before cooking or until chunks smolder. Meanwhile, rub turkey breast with garlic and then sprinkle with salt and pepper. Insert rotisserie rod through turkey breast and tighten spit forks at both ends of rod and test for balance, readjusting if necessary. Place rod on grill. Put drip pan directly under turkey on grill. Turn on spit and cook, covered, for about 1½ hours, basting with butter every 20-25 minutes, and replenishing hickory chunks as necessary. Allow turkey to stand for 10 minutes before carving.

Makes about 12 servings.

gingered turkey drumsticks

Turkey drumsticks make handy finger food especially good for picnics.

¼ cup	medium dry sherry
2 tablespoons	honey
2 tablespoons	rice wine vinegar
4 teaspoons	soy sauce
½ teaspoon	dry mustard
2 tablespoons	minced scallion
½ teaspoon	grated fresh ginger root
4	turkey drumsticks (2½ to 3 lb.)

In a bowl, stir together sherry, honey, vinegar, soy, mustard, scallion and ginger root. Place drumsticks on grill over low heat. Baste with sherry mixture; cover grill. Continue cooking and basting, turning periodically, for about 45 minutes or until drumsticks are cooked.

Makes 4 servings.

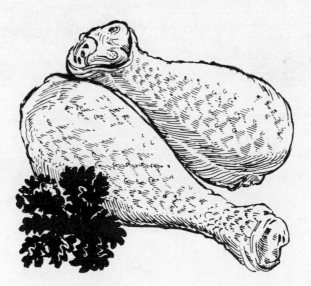

lamb and veal

butterflied leg of lamb

The grill basket makes simple work of turning and basting the leg of lamb.

¼ cup	dry vermouth or dry white wine
2 tablespoons	vegetable oil
1 tablespoon	lemon juice
2	garlic cloves, minced
1 teaspoon	dried rosemary leaves
1	leg of lamb, butterflied

In a bowl, stir together vermouth, oil, lemon juice, garlic and rosemary. Pour mixture into large plastic bag. Place lamb in bag with marinade and seal well. Turn bag so that meat is well coated with marinade. Refrigerate for at least 6-8 hours, turning periodically. To cook, place lamb in grill basket. Put on grill over low heat and cook, covered, for about 45 minutes, turning and basting with marinade periodically. Using meat thermometer test lamb for doneness. Meat is medium rare at 140°F. Allow lamb to rest for 5 minutes before carving.

Makes 8-10 servings.

delicious main dishes

stuffed leg of lamb

Rotisserie lamb makes a wonderful presentation for a special occasion.

1½ cups	chopped scallion
3 tablespoons	vegetable oil
4½ cups	soft bread crumbs
¼ cup	milk
4½ tablespoons	chopped fresh mint, divided
2 tablespoons	finely chopped lemon rind
1½ teaspoons	salt
½ teaspoon	ground pepper
1	boned leg of lamb (5½ to 6 lbs.) ready for stuffing
4	garlic cloves, minced
⅓ cup	olive oil
1 tablespoon	lemon juice

In a fry pan, sautée scallion in vegetable oil over moderate heat until soft; set aside. In a bowl, stir together bread crumbs, milk, 3 tablespoons mint, lemon rind, salt, pepper, and scallion with oil. Stuff mixture into pocket of lamb; tie lamb to secure stuffing. Insert rotisserie rod lengthwise through center of meat. Balance roast and tighten spit forks to fasten meat securely so that it turns only with the rod. In a bowl, stir together garlic, olive oil, lemon juice and remaining mint. Place rotisserie rod on grill and cook meat over low flame in covered grill, basting periodically with seasoned oil, for about 50 minutes (for rare meat internal temperature will be about 140°F.; 160°F. for medium; 170°F. for well-done). Allow meat to rest for 10 minutes before carving.

Makes about 12 servings.

roast rack of lamb

So that ends of rib bones don't burn, cover them with aluminum foil.

⅓ cup	vegetable oil
2	garlic cloves, minced
1 teaspoon	dried rosemary leaves
1 teaspoon	salt
¼ teaspoon	ground pepper
1	rack of lamb (8 rib)

In a bowl, stir together oil, garlic, rosemary, salt and pepper. Place lamb on Step-Up-Grid of grill. Baste with seasoned oil. Cook in covered grill over low heat for 40 minutes, basting periodically. Check for desired doneness with meat thermometer. (Internal temperature will be 165°F. for medium; 170-180°F. for well done.) Allow lamb to rest for about 5 minutes before carving.

Makes 4 servings.

apricot lamb kebobs

The combination of apricot sweetness and garlic-onion spiciness makes a succulent combination with lamb.

¼ cup	chopped onion
1	garlic clove, minced
2 tablespoons	vegetable oil
12	dried apricot halves
1 can (5½ oz.)	apricot nectar
2 tablespoons	water
2 teaspoons	cider vinegar
1 tablespoon	brown sugar
1 teaspoon	salt
¼ teaspoon	ground pepper
1½ lbs.	boneless lamb, cut into 1-inch cubes
	metal or wooden skewers

In a small saucepan, cook onion and garlic in oil until tender. Remove from heat and pour into cup of blender or food processor. Add apricot halves, apricot nectar, water, vinegar, sugar, salt and pepper. Purée. Pour baste into bowl. Thread lamb on skewers; place on grill. Baste with sauce. Grill over medium to high heat in covered grill, basting and turning occasionally. Cook for about 10-15 minutes or until meat reaches desired degree of doneness.

Makes 6 servings.

garlicky shish kebobs

If you prefer less garlic, reduce the amount to 1 garlic clove only. The marinade otherwise will be in balance.

⅓ cup	red wine vinegar
¼ cup	vegetable oil
3	garlic cloves, minced
2 tablespoons	Worcestershire sauce
1 teaspoon	salt
4 drops	hot red pepper sauce
1½ lbs.	boneless lamb, cut into 1-inch cubes
12	mushroom caps
12	cherry tomatoes
2	medium green peppers, seeded and cut into chunks
1	onion, peeled and cut into chunks
	metal or wooden skewers

In a bowl, stir together vinegar, oil, garlic, Worcestershire sauce, salt and pepper sauce. Pour into large plastic bag. Place lamb in bag and seal well. Turn bag so that meat is well coated with marinade. Allow to marinate for 2 hours at room temperature or 4-6 hours refrigerated. Remove meat from marinade and thread on skewers alternately with mushrooms, tomatoes, peppers and onion. Place on grill. Cook over medium heat in covered grill for about 15-20 minutes, turning periodically.

Makes 6 servings.

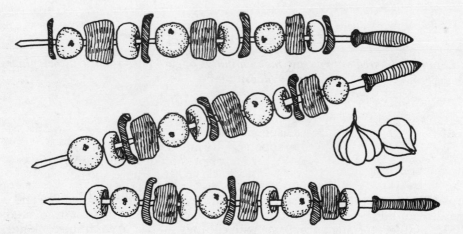

mustard-coated lamb chops

Be sure that chops are well trimmed of fat.

2 tablespoons	prepared Dijon mustard
2 tablespoons	soy sauce
3 tablespoons	lemon juice
2 tablespoons	vegetable oil
8	rib or shoulder lamb chops

In a bowl, beat together mustard, soy, lemon juice and oil. Place chops on grill over medium to high heat. Baste with mustard sauce. Cover grill and cook for about 15 minutes for medium done chops, turning and basting periodically with mustard sauce. Increase cooking time for more well done meat.

Makes 4 servings.

chutney lamb chops

Chops are basted only during last 5 minutes of cooking so that chutney glaze doesn't burn.

1 cup	chutney
¼ cup	water
4 teaspoons	lemon juice
2 teaspoons	dry mustard
8	rib or shoulder lamb chops, cut (1½ inches thick)

In cup of blender or food processor, purée chutney with water, lemon juice and mustard. Pour into bowl. Place chops on grill and cook over high heat in covered grill for 10-12 minutes, turning once. Baste with chutney glaze and continue cooking, turning once and basting, for 5 minutes. Check for doneness and continue cooking if desired.

Makes 4 servings.

mixed grill

A mixed grill is simply a combination of a few broiled meats, vegetables and perhaps, fruit. Let your imagination help you select other combinations of ingredients.

4	rib or shoulder lamb chops (1-inch thick)
3	fresh peaches, peeled and quartered
12	fresh mushroom caps
8	pork sausages
	metal or wooden skewers
3 tablespoons	vegetable oil
1 teaspoon	salt
¼ teaspoon	ground pepper

Thread chops, peach quarters, mushrooms and sausages alternately on skewers. Brush with oil and sprinkle with salt and pepper. Place on grill and cook, covered, for about 10-15 minutes, turning once. Check for desired doneness, cooking longer if desired.

Makes 4 servings.

zesty barbecued lamb riblets

Dijon mustard spices up the tomatoey barbecue sauce.

1 cup	chili sauce
6 tablespoons	water
1½ tablespoons	Dijon mustard
3 lbs.	lamb riblets

In a bowl, stir together chili sauce, water and Dijon mustard. Place lamb riblets on grill over low heat and baste with sauce. Cook in covered grill for about 20-25 minutes, turning and basting periodically.

Makes 4 servings.

barbecued lamb shanks with tomato-wine sauce

This inexpensive cut of meat is simply prepared and delicious when grilled.

1 can (8 oz.)	tomato sauce
¾ cup	dry white wine
2 tablespoons	lemon juice
2 tablespoons	vegetable oil
1½ tablespoons	Worcestershire sauce
¼ cup	finely chopped onion
2	garlic cloves, minced
1	bay leaf, crumbled
1 teaspoon	salt
¼ teaspoon	ground pepper
6	lamb shanks

In a saucepan over moderate heat, cook tomato sauce, wine, lemon juice, oil, Worcestershire sauce, onion, garlic, bay leaf, salt and pepper for 30 minutes, stirring occasionally. Remove from heat and cool. Pour liquid into large plastic bag. Place lamb shanks in bag, seal well and turn bag so that lamb is well coated with marinade. Let stand at room temperature for at least 3-4 hours. Place lamb shanks on grill over low heat. Cover grill and cook for about 30 minutes, turning and basting periodically with marinade.

Makes 6 servings.

veal chops with wine shallot butter

Carefully time the cooking of veal chops. If they are at all overcooked they will be very dry.

¼ cup	butter or margarine
3 tablespoons	finely chopped scallion
1 tablespoon	white wine
¼ teaspoon	salt
4	veal chops, cut 1½ inches thick

In a small saucepan, melt butter; add scallion and cook for 3-5 minutes. Remove from heat and stir in wine and salt. Place chops on grill and baste with butter. Cook over low heat in covered grill for about 15 minutes, turning and basting at least twice during cooking.

Makes 4 servings.

spinach-stuffed veal cutlets

Turkey cutlets may also be used for this recipe.

1 package (10 oz.)	fresh spinach, cooked and finely chopped
10 tablespoons	grated Parmesan cheese, divided
¼ teaspoon	salt
¼ teaspoon	ground pepper
⅛ teaspoon	ground nutmeg
1 lb.	veal cutlets, pounded until thin
1	egg
2 tablespoons	chopped parsley
6 tablespoons	butter or margarine, melted

In a bowl, stir together spinach, 2 tablespoons cheese, salt, pepper and nutmeg. Spread a spoonful of spinach mixture at one edge of each cutlet and roll up cutlet. Secure with food pick. In a shallow bowl, stir together remaining cheese with parsley. In another bowl, beat egg. Dip rolled cutlets first into egg and then into cheese mixture. Brush well with butter and place on grill over low heat. Cook for 10-15 minutes, basting periodically with butter and turning until well-browned on all sides.

Makes 4 servings.

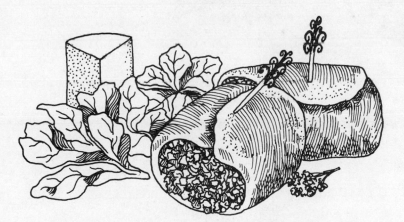

fish and seafood

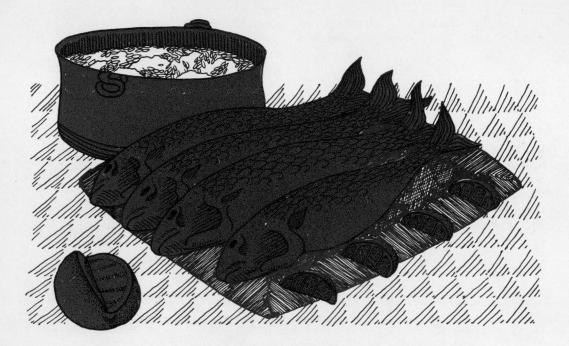

crumbed fish fillets

Using a grill basket will make the fish very easy to handle and turn.

⅔ cup	fine dry bread crumbs
1 tablespoon	chopped parsley
2 teaspoons	grated lemon rind
1 teaspoon	salt
½ teaspoon	crushed fennel seeds
½ teaspoon	ground pepper
6 tablespoons	butter or margarine, melted
2 lbs.	fish fillets

In a bowl, stir together crumbs, parsley, lemon rind, salt, fennel seeds and pepper. Pour butter into a shallow bowl or plate. Dip fish fillets first into butter and then into seasoned crumbs. Place fish in grill basket and place basket on grill. Cook over low heat in covered grill for about 15-20 minutes, turning every 5 minutes. Cooking time will depend upon thickness of fish fillets.

Makes 6 servings.

delicious main dishes

cheesy fish fingers

Select a fish like halibut, swordfish or schrod for this recipe because it will be firm enough to hold its shape on the grill.

½ cup	grated Parmesan cheese
½ cup	cornflake crumbs
¼ teaspoon	ground pepper
½ cup	butter or margarine, melted
1 lb.	firm-flesh fish as halibut, swordfish or schrod
	wooden or metal skewers

In a shallow bowl, stir together cheese, crumbs and pepper. Pour butter into another shallow bowl. Cut fish into finger-shape sticks about 3-inches long. Dip fish fingers first into butter and then roll in cheese-crumb mixture. Place skewer through fish fingers lengthwise. Place fish on grill over low heat and cook, covered, for about 5-7 minutes per side until lightly browned.

Makes 4 servings.

fillet of sole with mushrooms

This very simple fish recipe is low in calories, too.

2 teaspoons	butter or margarine
1 lb.	fillets of sole
1 teaspoon	salt
¼ teaspoon	ground pepper
4 teaspoons	lemon juice
¼ cup	dry vermouth
1½ cups	fresh sliced mushrooms
	aluminum foil

Butter centers of 4 strips of aluminum foil. Sprinkle fillets with salt and pepper; roll up each fillet. Place fillets in portions on foil strips. Top each serving with lemon juice, vermouth and mushrooms. Seal sole carefully in foil. Place on grill over low heat. Close grill cover and cook for 20 minutes.

Makes 4 servings.

fish steaks with onion

Bermuda onions give this dish a hint of sweetness.

3 tablespoons	butter or margarine
1 lb.	Bermuda onion, peeled and very thinly sliced
½ teaspoon	salt
¼ teaspoon	ground pepper
	aluminum foil

Melt butter in fry pan over moderate heat. Add onions and cook for about 15 minutes or until onions are tender and golden brown. Stir in salt and pepper. Place each fish steak in aluminum foil pouch. Top with onions and seal pouches securely. Place on grill over low heat. Cook in covered grill for 15-20 minutes.

Makes 4 servings.

halibut tomato packets

When fresh tomatoes are not available, canned tomatoes give a fuller flavor.

4	halibut steaks (5-6 oz., each)
3	medium tomatoes, peeled, seeded and chopped
1	small onion, finely chopped
1 teaspoon	dried leaf basil
1½ teaspoons	salt
¼ teaspoon	ground pepper
2 tablespoons	butter or margarine, melted
	aluminum foil

Make 4 pouches of aluminum foil. Place a halibut steak in each. Top each steak with tomato, onion, basil, salt, pepper and butter. Wrap foil securely around fish. Place on grill over low heat in covered grill and cook for 20-25 minutes.

Makes 4 servings.

marinated flounder and onions

Here the fish and onions are marinated together and served together, but cooked separately.

⅓ cup	vegetable oil
⅓ cup	white wine vinegar
1	garlic clove, minced
1 tablespoon	chopped parsley
1 teaspoon	salt
½ teaspoon	dried oregano leaves
¼ teaspoon	ground pepper
1½ lbs.	flounder or halibut steak, cut into 1½-inch cubes
1	small Bermuda onion, thinly sliced

In a bowl, stir together oil, vinegar, garlic, parsley, salt, oregano and pepper. Add fish cubes to marinade and toss to coat well. In another bowl, arrange ½ of the onions in a layer. Place fish on top of onions; cover with another layer of onions. Pour marinade over all ingredients. Cover and refrigerate for 2 hours. Thread fish onto skewers and place on grill. Wrap onion slices securely in aluminum foil and place on grill. Cook both over low heat in covered grill for about 10-15 minutes, basting fish periodically with marinade. Serve fish with onions.

Makes 4 servings.

swordfish kebobs

To save last minute preparation, fish and vegetables may be placed on skewers several hours before cooking. Just wrap kebobs well and refrigerate them.

1 lb.	fresh swordfish steak, cut into 1-inch chunks
2	fresh limes, cut into eighths
12	cherry tomatoes
10	scallions, cut into 2-inch pieces
	metal or wooden skewers
¼ cup	butter or margarine, melted
2 tablespoons	lemon juice
1 tablespoon	chopped parsley
¼ teaspoon	salt
⅛ teaspoon	ground pepper

Alternate pieces of fish, lime, tomato and scallion on skewers. In a small bowl, stir together butter, lemon juice, parsley, salt and pepper. Place kebobs on grill and baste with seasoned butter. Cook over low heat in covered grill for about 5 minutes per side, basting periodically during cooking.

Makes 4 servings.

salmon with dill mustard sauce

Fresh dill is essential to the flavor of this recipe.

2 lbs.	center cut fresh salmon
1 bunch	fresh dill
¼ cup	prepared dark mustard
3 tablespoons	cider vinegar
2 tablespoons	vegetable oil
1 tablespoon	sugar

Chop enough dill to make 1½ tablespoons; set aside. Place remaining dill in the cavity and around the sides of salmon and place fish on plate, cover, and refrigerate for about 6 hours.

In a bowl, stir together mustard, vinegar, oil, sugar and chopped dill.

To cook, remove dill from salmon and place salmon in grill basket. Baste with mustard mixture and cook in covered grill over low heat for about 15 minutes per side, basting periodically.

Makes 4 servings.

cod steak with beurre blanc

Beurre blanc, a flavored butter, should be made just before serving.

4	cod steaks (about ¾-inch thick)
1 tablespoon	vegetable oil
¼ cup	white wine vinegar
¼ cup	dry white wine
1 tablespoon	lemon juice
3 tablespoons	finely minced shallot or scallion
Few grindings	white pepper
1 cup	unsalted butter, cut into very small pieces

Brush fish with oil and place on grill over low heat. Cook in covered grill for about 10 minutes per side. In a saucepan, simmer vinegar, wine, lemon juice, shallot and pepper over moderate heat until reduced to 1 tablespoon. Remove from heat and cool slightly. Whisk butter, one piece at a time, into liquid. Continue with remaining butter. Sauce will become thick like a hollandaise sauce. Spoon onto cooked fish and serve immediately.

Makes 4 servings.

orange-basted salmon steaks

If salmon steaks are not available, salmon fillets will work just as well.

4	salmon steaks (6 oz., each)
½ can (6 oz.)	frozen orange juice concentrate
4 teaspoons	soy sauce
1	garlic clove, minced

Place salmon steaks on grill. In a small bowl, stir together orange juice, soy and garlic; baste salmon steaks with this mixture. Cook over low heat in covered grill for about 20 minutes, turning and basting every 5 minutes during cooking.

Makes 4 servings.

halibut steak with dill caper butter

Try the flavored butter with other grilled fish fillets or steaks.

3 tablespoons	butter or margarine
1½ teaspoons	fresh chopped dill weed
2 teaspoons	capers
¼ teaspoon	ground pepper
1	halibut steak (about 1½ lbs.)

In a small saucepan, melt butter. Remove from heat and stir in dill, capers and pepper. Place halibut steak on grill over low to medium heat. Baste with seasoned butter. Cover grill and cook for about 10 minutes per side, turning and basting periodically during cooking.

Makes 4-6 servings.

delicious main dishes

rice-stuffed mackerel

Have fishmonger remove heads and insides of fish.

1 tablespoon	vegetable oil
1	small onion, chopped
¼ cup	converted rice
½ cup	water
½ teaspoon	fennel seed, crushed
¼ teaspoon	salt
1 tablespoon	lemon juice
⅛ teaspoon	ground pepper
2	whole mackerel (about 1 lb., each)

Pour oil into saucepan and place over moderate heat. Sauté onion in oil until tender, not browned. Add rice and cook for 2 minutes. Stir in water, fennel seed, salt, lemon juice and pepper. Cover and cook according to directions on rice package. Fill cavity of fish with cooked rice. Tie fish to hold in filling. Place fish in grill basket and put on grill over low heat. Cook for 30 minutes, turning at least twice during cooking.

Makes 4 servings.

grilled whole trout

Slashing the fish flesh with a knife and marinating gives the trout a very full flavor.

6	whole pan-dressed rainbow or brook trout (about 8 oz. each)
1 bottle (8 oz.)	Caesar salad dressing
2 tablespoons	chopped parsley

With a sharp knife, make 3 light slashes on each side of fish. Pour dressing into 13 x 9-inch baking pan; stir in parsley. Place fish in dressing, turning over to coat with marinade. Cover and refrigerate for 3-4 hours, turning at least twice. Remove fish from marinade and place in grill basket. Cook over medium heat in covered grill, basting frequently with marinade. Cook for about 10 minutes or until fish flakes easily with a fork.

Makes 6 servings.

wine-steamed mussels

Soak mussels for an hour in cold water to insure easy cleaning.

1 cup	dry white wine
1	small onion, chopped
1	garlic clove, minced
2 tablespoons	lemon juice
2 tablespoons	chopped parsley
2 lbs.	fresh mussels, cleaned and drained
	aluminum foil

Place wine, onion, garlic, lemon juice and parsley in 2-3-inch deep metal cooking pan. Place mussels in pan and wrap tightly in a double layer of aluminum foil. Place wrapped mussels on grill above medium high heat. Cover grill and cook for about 10 minutes or until wine comes to a boil and mussels open. Serve immediately.

Makes 4 servings as an appetizer or 2 servings as entrée.

steamed clams

Cooking clams on the grill is every bit as easy as preparing them on the stove.

4 lbs.	fresh clams
½ cup	butter or margarine, melted
	aluminum foil

Rinse clams thoroughly and place in metal pan. Pour 1 cup water into pan; cover with aluminum foil, sealing edges well. Place pan on grill over medium heat. Close grill cover and cook for about 10 minutes or until water has boiled and clams have opened. Serve with melted butter.

Makes 4 servings.

scampi en brochette

If large shrimp are unavailable or too expensive, substitute medium-sized or smaller shrimp.

5 tablespoons	olive oil
5	garlic cloves, minced
3 tablespoons	lemon juice
2 tablespoons	minced shallot or green onion
2 tablespoons	chopped parsley
½ teaspoon	ground pepper
16	large raw peeled and deveined shrimp (1½ lbs.)
	metal or wooden skewers

In a shallow bowl, stir together oil, garlic, lemon juice, shallot, parsley and pepper. Add shrimp to seasoned oil and allow to marinate for 1 hour. Thread shrimp onto skewers and place on grill over low heat; cover grill. Cook for about 20 minutes, turning and basting with marinade periodically during cooking.

Makes 4 servings.

scallops and shrimp with fresh tomatoes

Skins can be easily peeled if tomatoes are dipped in boiling water for about 15 seconds.

¾ cup	chopped onion
¼ cup	chopped green pepper
1	garlic clove, minced
3	medium tomatoes, peeled, seeded and chopped
2 tablespoons	dry vermouth
1 tablespoon	chopped parsley
1 teaspoon	salt
¼ teaspoon	ground pepper
1 lb.	scallops
½ lb.	medium shrimp, peeled
	aluminum foil

In a fry pan over moderate heat, cook onion, peppers and garlic in oil until vegetables are tender. Stir in tomatoes, vermouth, parsley, salt and pepper and continue cooking for an additional 5 minutes. Make 4 foil pouches. Divide scallops and shrimp among pouches. Spoon vegetables into each pouch. Fold foil and seal well. Place pouches on grill over low heat and cook, covered, for about 15-20 minutes.

Makes 4 servings.

scallops en brochette

If scallops are large, simply cut them in half for quicker cooking.

28	cherry tomatoes, washed and stems removed
1 lb.	fresh scallops
14 strips	bacon, cut in half lengthwise
	metal or wooden skewers

Baste:

¼ cup	soy sauce
¼ cup	lemon juice
6 tablespoons	lime juice
½ teaspoon	salt

Arrange skewers with cherry tomatoes at each end and scallops in the centers interspersed with bacon strips. In a bowl, stir together soy, lemon juice and lime juice. Place scallops on grill rack over low to medium heat and baste with juice mixture. Turn and baste periodically during cooking. Cook in covered grill for about 10 minutes.

Makes 4 servings.

linguini with clam sauce

The recipe calls for cherrystone clams, though little neck clams or other fresh clams may be substituted.

2 dozen	cherrystone clams
3 tablespoons	butter or margarine
2	garlic cloves, minced
1 package (8 oz.)	linguini
2 tablespoons	chopped parsley
¼ cup	grated Parmesan cheese
	aluminum foil

Wash clams. Make pouch of double layer of aluminum foil; place clams in pouch. In a small saucepan over moderate heat, melt butter; add garlic and cook for about 3-5 minutes; remove from heat. Pour garlic butter over clams. Seal foil securely around clams; place on grill. Cook clams over low heat for about 10 minutes or until they open. Meanwhile cook linguini according to package directions in salted boiling water. Serve clams over linguini; sprinkle with parsley and cheese.

Makes 4 servings.

king crab legs with lemon-wine butter

Because frozen crab legs have been previously cooked, the preparation of this recipe is very fast.

¼ cup	butter or margarine
6 tablespoons	dry white wine
¼ cup	lemon juice
2 tablespoons	minced scallion
¼ teaspoon	ground pepper
2 lbs.	king crab legs
	aluminum foil

In a small saucepan, melt butter. Stir in wine, lemon juice, scallion and pepper; cook for 2 minutes over low heat. With a sharp knife, split crab legs horizontally; place crab on double thickness of aluminum foil. Pour seasoned butter over cut side of crab legs. Carefully fold and seal foil around crab. Place on grill rack over low heat and cook, covered, for 10-15 minutes.

Makes 4 servings.

broiled lobster

Simple and delicious! Just grill and serve with melted butter.

4 live lobsters (about 1 lb., each)
¼ cup butter, melted

Request split and cleaned lobsters. Crack large part of each claw with mallet. Brush cut surface of lobster with butter and place cut-side-down on grill. Cook over medium heat for about 10 minutes. Serve with additional melted butter.

Makes 4 servings.

vegetables/fruits

au gratin potatoes

To take best advantage of the grill, plan to cook the potatoes alongside the entrée.

2 teaspoons	vegetable oil
6	medium baking potatoes, peeled and thinly sliced
4 tablespoons	butter or margarine
1½ teaspoons	salt
¼ teaspoon	ground pepper
2 cups	shredded cheddar cheese
	paprika
	aluminum foil

Spread oil on center of aluminum foil strip. Arrange ¼ of the potato slices on foil. Sprinkle with ¼ each salt, pepper, paprika and cheese. Dot with butter. Repeat layers with remaining ingredients, ending with butter. Wrap foil around potatoes and seal well. Place on grill over low heat, cover grill and cook for 1 hour.

Makes 4-6 servings.

fine on the side

baked stuffed potatoes

This is a good vegetable to serve when you are planning to use the grill for a long time to cook other foods.

8	baking potatoes, scrubbed
	aluminum foil
1 package (8 oz.)	garlic and herb cheese
1 stick (8 tablespoons)	butter or margarine, melted
2 tablespoons	milk
1 teaspoon	salt
¼ teaspoon	ground pepper

Put potatoes in metal pan and wrap in foil. Place on grill over low heat and cook in covered grill for about 40 minutes or until soft. Remove slice from top of potatoes and carefully scoop out inside into a large bowl, leaving potato skin shell. Set shells aside. Mash potato with cheese, butter, milk, salt and pepper. Refill shells with mashed potato mixture. Return potatoes to metal pan and re-wrap in foil. Place on Step-Up-Grid and cook for 15-20 minutes or until warm.

Makes 8 servings.

potato slices in foil

To vary the shape, potatoes may be cut into sticks.

4	medium baking potatoes, unpeeled
6 tablespoons	butter or margarine, softened
¼ teaspoon	dried leaf thyme
⅛ teaspoon	ground nutmeg
⅛ teaspoon	instant minced onion
⅛ teaspoon	ground pepper
	aluminum foil

Cut each potato into ½-inch thick slices. In a bowl, cream butter with thyme, nutmeg, onion and pepper. Spread butter between potato slices. Wrap each potato separately in foil, sealing well. Place on Step-Up-Grid over low heat in covered grill. Cook for 1 hour. Remove from foil and serve.

Makes 4 servings.

green and wax beans with onion

All green beans or wax beans may be used in this recipe.

3 tablespoons	butter or margarine, divided
1 lb.	fresh green beans, washed and trimmed
1 lb.	fresh wax beans, washed and trimmed
1	small red onion, peeled and very thinly sliced
¼ teaspoon	ground pepper

Butter center of piece of aluminum foil. Arrange layers of green beans, wax beans and onions on foil, sprinkling layers with salt and pepper. Continue with layers until beans, onions and seasonings are used. Dot top with butter. Seal well in a double layer of foil and place on Step-Up-Grid over low heat. Cook for 15-20 minutes or until beans are tender.

Makes 6 servings.

corn with green onion

An easy to eat recipe for fresh summer corn.

6 ears	fresh corn, husked
¾ cup	chopped scallion
1 teaspoon	salt
¼ teaspoon	ground pepper
2 tablespoons	butter or margarine
	aluminum foil

Cut corn from the cob and place in large bowl. Stir in scallion, salt and pepper. Spoon corn onto double thickness of aluminum foil. Dot top with butter. Carefully fold and seal foil around corn. Place on Step-Up-Grid of grill and cook, covered, over low heat for about 20-25 minutes.

Makes 6 servings.

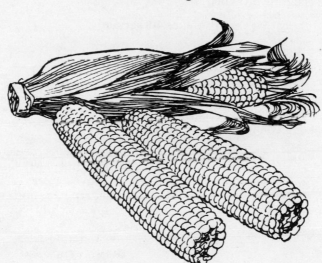

grilled eggplant with garlic

Select an eggplant that has a smooth outside and is firm.

1	medium eggplant (about 1½ lbs.), peeled
1 tablespoon	salt
⅓ cup	vegetable oil
2 tablespoons	lemon juice
2 tablespoons	chopped parsley
2	garlic cloves, minced

Cut eggplant horizontally into 1-inch thick slices; place on baking sheet and sprinkle both sides of eggplant with salt. Allow to stand for 30 minutes; rinse and drain well.

In a bowl, stir together oil, lemon juice, parsley and garlic. Place eggplant slices on grill over low to medium heat. Baste with oil mixture. Turn and baste during cooking until eggplant is lightly browned.

Makes 4-6 servings.

ratatouille in foil

Ratatouille can be varied by the addition of other kinds of summer squashes and mushrooms.

2 tablespoons	vegetable oil
2	medium onions, peeled and sliced
1	green pepper, seeded and sliced
2	garlic cloves, peeled and minced
¾ lb.	eggplant, peeled and cut into 2-inch sticks
1	medium zucchini, cut into 2-inch sticks
1 tablespoon	salt
1 can (16 oz.)	whole tomatoes, drained and coarsely chopped
¼ teaspoon	ground pepper
	aluminum foil

In a fry pan over moderate heat, cook onions, pepper and garlic in oil. When tender, remove from heat. Meanwhile spread eggplant and zucchini on baking sheet and sprinkle with salt. Allow to stand for 30 minutes, rinse and drain thoroughly. In a pouch made of a double layer of foil, stir together onion mixture with eggplant, zucchini, tomatoes and pepper. Seal pouch thoroughly and place on grill over low heat. Cook for 30 minutes.

Makes 4-6 servings.

cherry tomatoes with basil

Watch the cooking time on this recipe. The tomatoes are better undercooked than overcooked.

3 tablespoons	butter or margarine, divided
40 (1 lb.)	cherry tomatoes, trimmed and washed
1 teaspoon	dried basil leaves
½ teaspoon	salt
⅛ teaspoon	ground pepper
	aluminum foil

Butter center of aluminum foil strip with ½ tablespoon butter. Place tomatoes on foil. Dot with remaining butter and sprinkle with basil, salt and pepper. Fold foil over tomatoes and seal well. Place foil packet on grill over low heat. Cook for 10-15 minutes.

Makes 8 servings.

escalloped tomatoes

There's no better way to take advantage of the seasonal abundance of garden tomatoes.

3 tablespoons	butter or margarine, divided
6	medium tomatoes, sliced ½-inch thick
1	small onion, finely chopped
¼ cup	grated Parmesan cheese
2 teaspoons	dried basil leaves
1 teaspoon	salt
½ teaspoon	ground pepper
	aluminum foil

Spread center of double layer of aluminum foil with ½ tablespoon butter. Top with ⅓ tomato slices, sprinkle with ⅓ each of cheese, basil, salt and pepper. Repeat layers, ending with pepper. Dot top with remaining butter. Seal foil around tomatoes. Place tomatoes on Step-Up-Grid over low heat in covered grill and cook for 20-30 minutes.

Makes 6 servings.

squash kebobs with garlic butter

Other summer vegetables like tomato and pepper can easily be added to the skewers.

¼ cup	butter or margarine
3	garlic cloves, minced
1 tablespoon	chopped parsley
¼ teaspoon	ground pepper
2	medium zuccini, cut into 1½-inch thick pieces
2	medium summer squash, cut into 1½-inch thick pieces
	metal or wooden skewers

Over low heat, melt butter in a small saucepan. Add garlic and cook for 3-5 minutes. Stir in parsley and pepper. Thread zucchini and summer squash alternately onto skewers. Place on grill over low to medium heat. Baste with flavored butter; cover grill and cook. Baste with butter and turn periodically while cooking for about 15-20 minutes or until tender.

Makes 4-6 servings.

mushrooms on skewer

An herb butter baste flavors these mushrooms.

6 tablespoons	butter or margarine
2 tablespoons	minced chives
1 teaspoon	dried rosemary leaves
¼ teaspoon	ground black pepper
32	medium fresh mushroom caps, washed and trimmed
	wooden or metal skewers

In a small saucepan, melt butter over moderate heat. Stir in chives, rosemary and pepper; remove from heat and set aside. Arrange mushroom caps on skewers; place on grill over low heat. Baste with seasoned butter. Cook, covered, for 5-10 minutes, basting and turning periodically.

Makes 4 servings.

grilled onions

Versatile onions are exceptionally good when grilled until lightly browned.

4	Bermuda onions, peeled
¼ cup	vegetable oil
2 tablespoons	sesame oil
1 teaspoon	salt
¼ teaspoon	ground pepper
1 tablespoon	parsley

Cut each onion into 4-5 thick slices. In a small bowl, stir together oils, salt, pepper and parsley. Place onion slices on grill over low to medium heat. Baste with oil mixture. Cook for 5-10 minutes, basting and turning periodically until onions are lightly browned.

Makes 4-6 servings.

stuffed artichokes

Opt for stuffed artichokes either as a first course or as a vegetable.

4	medium whole artichokes
1	medium onion, chopped
1	garlic clove, minced
6 tablespoons	vegetable oil
2 cups	soft, fresh bread crumbs
2 tablespoons	grated Parmesan cheese
2 teaspoons	dried basil leaves
1 teaspoon	salt
¼ teaspoon	ground pepper
	aluminum foil

Trim ends of artichoke leaves and cut off stems. Place in a large pot of rapidly boiling salted water. Cover pot and cook for about 30 minutes or until stem end pierces easily with a fork; drain. Meanwhile, prepare stuffing. In fry pan over moderate heat, cook onion and garlic in oil until soft, not browned. Add bread crumbs and continue cooking until bread is crisp, not browned; remove from heat. Stir in cheese, basil, salt and pepper.

When artichokes are cool enough to handle, use a spoon to scoop out thistle-like choke in center of each one. Spoon stuffing into centers. Press remaining stuffing between large outer leaves. Place stuffed artichokes on metal pie pan and cover with foil, sealing well. Place on Step-Up-Grid of grill, cover grill, and cook over low heat for about 35-40 minutes.

Makes 4 servings.

escalloped apples

This side dish may be cooked on the Step-Up-Grid at the same time the entrée is cooked.

6	medium apples, peeled, cored and sliced
¼ cup	butter or margarine, melted
3 tablespoons	honey
1 tablespoon	flour
½ teaspoon	grated nutmeg
¼ teaspoon	grated lemon rind
	aluminum foil

In a bowl, stir together apples, butter, honey, flour, nutmeg and lemon rind. Spoon into metal pie pan. Wrap pie pan in aluminum foil and place on Step-Up-Grid of grill. Cook over low heat for about 15 minutes or until apples are tender.

Makes 4-6 servings as side dish.

breads

fennel bread

Crush fennel seeds in blender cup, food processor, or with mortar and pestle.

1 loaf	French bread
6 tablespoons	butter or margarine, melted
1 tablespoon	chopped Italian parsley
1½ teaspoons	fennel seeds, crushed
	aluminum foil

Cut French bread every 2-3 inches almost through loaf. In a bowl, stir together butter, parsley and fennel. Spread flavored butter between slices of bread. Wrap loaf in foil and place on Step-Up-Grid over low heat. Warm for about 10 minutes in covered grill.

Makes 8-10 servings.

fine on the side

feta pocket bread

Semi-soft, mild cheese like Muenster or Monterey Jack may be substituted for feta cheese if you prefer.

3	loaves Syrian or pocket bread
1 cup	crumbled feta cheese
1 teaspoon	dried oregano leaves
	aluminum foil

Cut bread into quarters. In a small bowl, stir together cheese and oregano. Fill bread quarters with cheese mixture. Wrap filled bread in double thickness of aluminum foil and place on Step-Up-Grid of grill. Cover grill and warm over low heat for about 5-8 minutes.

Makes 12 servings.

cinnamon brown bread

Brown bread is available canned. Check next to the baked beans in your supermarket.

1 can (16 oz.)	brown bread with raisins
¼ cup	butter or margarine, softened
½ teaspoon	ground cinnamon
¼ teaspoon	ground nutmeg
	aluminum foil

Cut brown bread according to package directions into about 8-10 slices. In a bowl, cream together butter, cinnamon and nutmeg. Spread butter on each side of bread slices. Reassemble bread into a loaf and wrap in aluminum foil. Warm bread on Step-Up-Grid of covered grill over low heat for about 15 minutes.

Makes 8-10 servings.

italian toasted muffins

English muffins aren't for breakfast alone.

¼ cup	butter or margarine
1 teaspoon	dried oregano leaves
1 teaspoon	dried basil leaves
¼ teaspoon	instant minced garlic
4	English muffins, split

In a small saucepan, melt butter over low heat. Remove from heat and stir in oregano, basil and garlic. Brush English muffin halves with seasoned butter. Place muffins, buttered-side down on grill over high heat. Cook until muffins are toasted.

Makes 8 servings.

toasted bread sticks

These bread sticks are toasted on skewers for easy handling.

4	submarine or hoagie rolls
½ cup	butter or margarine, melted
2 tablespoons	chopped parsley
2 teaspoons	Summer Savory
	metal or wooden skewers

Cut rolls horizontally into 6 long wedges, each. In a small bowl, stir together butter, parsley and Summer Savory. Brush bread sticks with seasoned butter. Arrange bread sticks on skewers and place on grill rack over medium to high heat. Toast on each side until sticks are lightly browned.

Makes about 8 servings.

salads

savory potato salad

Prepared mustard spices up this version of potato salad.

4	medium potatoes, peeled and cubed
3 tablespoons	cider vinegar
1 package (10 oz.)	frozen green peas, cooked and drained
⅓ cup	finely chopped onion
¼ cup	mayonnaise
1½ tablespoons	prepared mustard
1 tablespoon	celery salt
1 tablespoon	milk or cream
1 teaspoon	salt
⅛ teaspoon	ground pepper

Cook potatoes in rapidly boiling salted water until tender; drain. Place in large bowl and immediately sprinkle with vinegar; cool. Add peas and onion. In a small bowl, stir together mayonnaise, mustard, celery salt, milk, salt and pepper. Pour over potatoes and toss well. Cover and chill.

Makes 4 servings.

fine on the side

tabbouleh

Get away from the traditional potato or macaroni salad by trying this one made with cracked wheat.

½ cup	finely cracked wheat or bulghur
3	tomatoes, chopped
1	medium onion, finely chopped
¼ cup	vegetable oil
¼ cup	lemon juice
½ cup	chopped parsley
2 tablespoons	finely chopped fresh mint
1½ teaspoons	salt

Place cracked wheat in bowl and add lukewarm water to cover. Allow to stand for 15 minutes until water is absorbed. Add tomatoes, onions, oil, lemon juice, parsley, mint and salt. Toss well and chill thoroughly. Serve on lettuce leaves.

Makes 4 servings.

pasta and proscuitto salad

Here's a salad with class - from appearance to flavor.

2 cups	rotini (corkscrew-shaped pasta)
1 ounce	very thinly sliced proscuitto
⅓ cup	chopped scallion
2 cups	broccoli flowerets, blanched and cooled
5 tablespoons	olive oil
3 tablespoons	wine vinegar
2 tablespoons	grated Parmesan cheese
2	garlic cloves, minced
½ teaspoon	salt
⅛ teaspoon	ground pepper

Cook pasta in rapidly boiling salted water according to package directions; drain and cool. Cut proscuitto into julienne strips about 2-inches long. In a large bowl, toss together cooked rotini, proscuitto, scallion, broccoli and cheese. In another bowl, beat together oil, vinegar, garlic, salt and pepper; pour as dressing over pasta mixture. Toss well. Cover salad and chill thoroughly. Toss again before serving.

Makes 6-8 servings.

chilled rice salad

Rice may also be cooked in beef broth, consommé, or any flavored stock.

1 cup	converted rice
3 cups	chicken broth
½ cup	minced onion
⅓ cup	pine nuts
5 tablespoons	vegetable oil, divided
¼ cup	chopped jarred red peppers
½ cup	chopped celery
3 tablespoons	cider vinegar
1 tablespoon	prepared mustard
1 teaspoon	salt
¼ teaspoon	ground pepper

Cook rice in chicken broth according to package directions; cool. Meanwhile in a frypan over moderate heat, cook onion and pine nuts in 1 tablespoon oil until tender; cool.

In a large bowl, stir together cooked rice, cooked onion and nuts, peppers and celery. In a small bowl, beat together remaining oil, vinegar, mustard, salt and pepper. Pour over rice mixture and toss well. Chill.

Makes 4-6 servings.

cabbage and pepper slaw

The colorful green pepper and carrot make this an attractive dish.

2½ cups	shredded cabbage(¾ lb.)
1	medium green pepper, seeded and very thinly sliced
1	carrot, peeled and shredded
¼ cup	mayonnaise
¼ cup	sour cream
1 tablespoon	cream or milk
1 tablespoon	cider vinegar
1 teaspoon	sugar
½ teaspoon	salt
⅛ teaspoon	ground pepper

In a large bowl, toss together cabbage, pepper and carrot. In a small bowl, stir together mayonnaise, sour cream, cream, vinegar, sugar, salt and pepper. Pour over cabbage mixture and toss well to coat vegetables. Cover and chill thoroughly.

Makes 4 servings.

seasonal salad

A delicious blend of colors and textures.

1	small head romaine, washed and torn into bite-size pieces
1	carrot, peeled and shredded
1 cup	bean sprouts
¼ cup	seedless raisins
1 cup	raw broccoli buds
¼ cup	slivered, toasted almonds

In a large bowl, toss together lettuce, carrots, sprouts, raisins, broccoli and almonds. Cover and chill until crisp. Toss with Herbed French Dressing or your favorite dressing.

Makes 4 servings.

herbed french dressing

Basil and tarragon flavor a classic French dressing.

¾ cup	olive oil
⅓ cup	wine vinegar
¾ teaspoon	salt
½ teaspoon	dried basil leaves
½ teaspoon	dried tarragon leaves
¾ teaspoon	salt
⅛ teaspoon	ground pepper

Place all ingredients in small bowl and beat well. Pour over green salad.

Makes about 1 cup dressing.

dilled carrots

A bright cold salad when you're tired of the usual marinated vegetables.

1 lb.	fresh carrots, peeled and cut diagonally into ½-inch thick slices
2 tablespoons	cider vinegar
3 tablespoons	oil
2 teaspoons	chopped parsley
1 teaspoon	dill weed
¼ teaspoon	salt
⅛ teaspoon	ground pepper

In a saucepan over moderate heat, cook carrots in rapidly boiling salted water until tender. Drain. Place carrots in a bowl and sprinkle with vinegar; cool. In a small bowl, stir together oil, parsley, dill weed, salt and pepper; pour over carrots and toss. Cover carrots and chill. Toss again just before serving.

Makes 4 servings.

orange, onion and walnut salad

The combination of ingredients, while unusual, is a delightful surprise of flavor and texture.

	lettuce leaves
4	medium oranges, peeled and sliced
1	medium red onion, peeled and thinly sliced
½ cup	walnuts, toasted and coarsely chopped
3 tablespoons	vegetable oil
2 tablespoons	lemon juice
½ teaspoon	dried leaf marjoram
¼ teaspoon	salt
⅛ teaspoon	ground pepper

Arrange lettuce leaves in a shallow bowl. Place orange slices and red onion on top of lettuce. Sprinkle with walnuts; chill. In a small bowl, beat together oil, lemon juice, marjoram, salt and pepper. Pour over oranges and onions.

Makes 4 servings.

eggplant salad

Though served chilled, this recipe begins by cooking eggplant on the grill.

2	medium eggplant (1½ lbs., each), peeled
4 teaspoons	salt, divided
7 tablespoons	vegetable oil, divided
2 tablespoons	red wine vinegar
¼ cup	chopped red onion
1 tablespoon	chopped fresh parsley
¼ teaspoon	ground pepper

Cut eggplant horizontally into ½-inch thick slices. Place slices on baking sheet and sprinkle both sides with 3 teaspoons salt. Allow to stand for 30 minutes; rinse and drain well. Brush eggplant slices with 4 tablespoons oil and place on grill over low heat. Cook until lightly browned on both sides.

Cut eggplant into julienne pieces about 2-inches by ½-inch and place in large bowl. Add vinegar, remaining salt, red onion, parsley and pepper; toss well. Cover salad and refrigerate for about 3 hours. Toss again before serving on lettuce leaves.

Makes 6-8 servings.

shredded zucchini salad

A delightful new way to serve zucchini.

1 lb.	fresh zucchini
1	small red onion, finely chopped
¼ cup	vegetable oil
2 tablespoons	red wine vinegar
1	garlic clove, minced
2 tablespoons	chopped parsley
½ teaspoon	fennel seed, crushed
½ teaspoon	salt
¼ teaspoon	ground pepper

Shred zucchini into a large bowl. Stir in red onion. In a small bowl, beat together oil, vinegar, garlic, parsley, fennel seed, salt and pepper. Pour over zucchini and toss. Chill thoroughly; toss again before spooning onto lettuce leaves to serve. Garnish with red onion rings.

Makes 4-6 servings.

green beans in tomato cups

This recipe looks bright and festive for any gathering.

1 lb.	fresh green beans, trimmed and cut into 1-inch pieces
8	medium tomatoes
¼ cup	vegetable oil
2½ tablespoons	wine vinegar
2 tablespoons	chopped chives
1	garlic clove, minced
¼ teaspoon	salt
¼ teaspoon	dry mustard
⅛ teaspoon	ground pepper

In a saucepan, cook beans in rapidly boiling salted water until just tender. Drain and cool immediately. Cut a thin slice from stem end of tomato and scoop out pulp from tomato, leaving shell. In a bowl, beat together oil, vinegar, chives, garlic, salt, mustard and pepper. Toss beans with oil dressing and refrigerate for 1-2 hours. Toss beans with dressing again and spoon into tomato·shells.

Makes 8 servings.

braised celery with green mayonnaise

This simple vegetable becomes elegant when topped with a flavorful homemade mayonnaise.

1 bunch	celery, trimmed
3 cups	chicken broth
1	egg
1 teaspoon	sugar
1 teaspoon	dry mustard
1 teaspoon	salt
⅔ cup	vegetable oil
8 sprigs	watercress
¼ cup	chopped pimiento

Cut celery into 4-inch chunks and then into wedges. Cook over low heat in chicken broth in shallow fry pan until tender. Drain and chill.

Meanwhile, in cup of blender or food processor, beat together egg, sugar, mustard and salt. Very gradually beat in oil in a thin stream. When dressing has thickened, add watercress and purée.

To serve, spoon watercress mayonnaise over braised celery and sprinkle with chopped pimiento.

Makes 4-6 servings.

sweet and sour beets

If you have time to let these beets marinate for 24 to 36 hours they will have even more flavor.

2	bunches fresh beets, trimmed, cooked and peeled
¼ cup	cider vinegar
2 tablespoons	honey
2 tablespoons	vegetable oil
½ teaspoon	salt
½ teaspoon	ground coriander
¼ teaspoon	ground clove
⅛ teaspoon	ground pepper

Cut beets in half and then slice. Place in bowl. In another bowl, stir together vinegar, honey, oil, salt, coriander, clove and pepper; pour over beets and toss well. Cover and refrigerate for at least 2 hours. Toss again before serving.

Makes 4-6 servings.

cauliflower remoulade

For a more elegant presentation, cook cauliflower as a whole head rather than breaking into flowerettes.

1	medium head cauliflower, trimmed and broken into flowerettes
½ cup	mayonnaise
4 teaspoons	caper juice
1 teaspoon	capers
1	garlic clove, minced
1 teaspoon	dried leaf tarragon
½ teaspoon	ground mustard
1 teaspoon	chopped fresh parsley

In a large saucepan, cook cauliflower in rapidly boiling salted water just until tender; drain and cool. Meanwhile, in a bowl, stir together mayonnaise, caper juice, capers, garlic, tarragon and mustard. To serve, spoon flavored mayonnaise over cooked cauliflower. Sprinkle with parsley.

Makes 6 servings.

cucumbers and tomatoes in sour cream

This salad is especially attractive when served on a bed of dark salad greens.

2	cucumbers, peeled
½ lb.	cherry tomatoes, halved
⅓ cup	sour cream
1 tablespoon	cider vinegar
1 teaspoon	dill weed
¼ teaspoon	salt
¼ teaspoon	grated onion
⅛ teaspoon	ground pepper

Halve cucumbers and remove seeds. Cut cucumbers into 1-inch slices and place in bowl. Add cherry tomatoes. In another bowl, stir together sour cream, vinegar, dill weed, salt, onion and pepper. Pour over cucumber-tomato mixture and toss well. Cover and chill for at least 1 hour before serving.

Makes 4 servings.

marinated chinese vegetable salad

Be sure to cook peapods only until tender-crisp and then cool immediately in cold water.

¾ cup	dried black Chinese mushrooms
1 lb.	fresh peapods, trimmed and halved
½ cup	sliced water chestnuts
3 tablespoons	vegetable oil
2 tablespoons	rice wine vinegar
2 teaspoons	sesame oil
1 teaspoon	soy sauce
3 drops	hot red pepper sauce
	salad greens

Rehydrate mushrooms in a bowl with boiling water; drain. Meanwhile, blanch peapods in rapidly boiling salted water; drain and cool. Slice mushrooms and place in bowl with peapods and water chestnuts. In another bowl, stir together vegetable oil, vinegar, sesame oil, soy sauce and pepper sauce. Pour over vegetables and toss well. Cover and refrigerate for 2 hours. Toss again and serve on salad greens.

Makes 4-6 servings.

happy endings

cold strawberry soufflé

Cold soufflés are attractive either in individual serving dishes or in a large soufflé dish.

2 teaspoons	vegetable oil
1 quart	fresh strawberries, washed and hulled
4	eggs
3	egg yolks
½ cup	sugar
2 envelopes (1 tablespoon, each)	unflavored gelatin
¼ cup	cold water
¼ cup	orange juice
3 tablespoons	Grand Marnier or cointreau, divided
2 cups	heavy cream, divided
¼ cup	confectioners' sugar
	aluminum foil

Using aluminum foil, prepare a 3-inch collar for a 5 to 6 cup soufflé dish. Brush inside of collar with vegetable oil and fasten collar well to dish with tape and/or string. In cup of blender or food processor, purée strawberries; set aside. In large bowl of mixer, beat eggs, egg yolks and sugar for 10 minutes or until mixture is very thick. In a small saucepan, sprinkle gelatin over cold water; let stand for 5 minutes until softened. Place saucepan over low heat and warm until gelatin is dissolved. Beat gelatin, orange juice and 2 tablespoons Grand Marnier into egg mixture. Add strawberry purée and beat at low speed until well mixed. In another bowl, beat 1 cup heavy cream until soft peaks form. Fold whipped cream into strawberry mixture. Pour into prepared soufflé dish and refrigerate for 6 hours.

In a bowl, whip remaining cream with confectioners' sugar and remaining Grand Marnier until stiff. Remove foil collar from soufflé dish and clean sides of dish. Decorate top of soufflé with whipped cream.

Makes about 8 servings.

strawberries with melba sauce

Fresh raspberries, if available, will improve the flavor of this recipe. Be sure to add a few tablespoons of sugar to the fresh purée to sweeten it a bit.

2 packages (10 oz., each)	frozen raspberries, thawed
1 teaspoon	grated orange rind
1 tablespoon	orange-flavored liqueur
1 quart	fresh strawberries, washed and hulled

Drain raspberries. Purée fruit in blender and strain out seeds. In a bowl, stir togther purée with orange rind and orange-flavored liqueur. Place strawberries in serving bowl(s); spoon melba sauce over strawberries.

Makes 4 servings.

strawberry rhubarb mousse

This recipe should be made in early summer when fresh rhubarb is available.

1 lb.	fresh rhubarb, trimmed and cut in chunks
½ cup	orange juice
½ cup	sugar
1	grated orange rind
1 pint	fresh strawberries, hulled and halved
3 tablespoons	orange-flavored liqueur
¾ cup	confectioners' sugar
1 cup	heavy cream
	red food coloring

In a saucepan over moderate heat, cook rhubarb in orange juice with sugar and orange rind until tender; remove from heat. Spoon rhubarb mixture into cup of blender or food processor and purée. Purée strawberries, too. In a bowl, stir together rhubarb and strawberry purées. Add liqueur. In another bowl, whip together confectioners' sugar and heavy cream; fold into strawberry-rhubarb purée. Add food coloring as desired. Pour into individual serving dishes and chill for at least 4 hours. Garnish, if desired, with additional whipped cream and strawberries.

Makes 6 servings.

strawberries with cassis sabayon

Crème de cassis, a black currant liqueur, replaces the marsala of a traditional saboyan sauce.

4	egg yolks
3 tablespoons	sugar
⅓ cup	crème de cassis
1 quart	fresh strawberries, hulled

In top of a double boiler, stir together egg yolks, sugar and crème de cassis. Place over hot water and beat continuously with electric mixer until mixture becomes thick and frothy. Spoon over servings of fresh strawberries.

Makes 4 servings.

melon in white wine

A dessert as simple as a splash of wine.

8 cups	cut up fresh melon (honeydew, cantaloupe, watermelon), chilled
1 cup	medium dry white wine, chilled
	fresh mint sprigs

Place melon in individual serving bowls. Pour some wine over each serving. Garnish each serving with mint sprig.

Makes 6 servings.

praline-chocolate ice cream bombe

Your favorite flavors of ice cream will make this molded ice cream dessert special.

1 quart	pecan praline ice cream, softened
1 quart	chocolate marshmallow ice cream, softened
½ pint	heavy cream
¼ cup	confectioners' sugar
1 teaspoon	vanilla extract
	pecan halves

Chill 6-cup to 8-cup gelatin mold in freezer. Spoon praline ice cream into mold to cover bottom and sides of mold well. Place in freezer for 30 minutes. Spoon chocolate ice cream into center of mold and return to freezer. Leave in freezer for several hours or until well frozen. To unmold, dip mold into pan of hot water and turn onto chilled serving plate; again return bombe to freezer. In a bowl, whip cream with confectioners' sugar and vanilla. Using a pastry bag, pipe whipped cream decoratively around bombe. Garnish with pecan halves. Cut into wedges to serve.

Makes 8-10 servings.

english toffee ice cream

You don't need an ice cream freezer to prepare this creamy smooth dessert.

1½ cups	milk
1 envelope (1 tablespoon)	plain gelatin
1 cup	sugar
3	egg yolks
1½ teaspoons	vanilla extract
4 (⅞ oz., each)	English toffee candy bars, crushed
1½ cups	heavy cream, whipped

Pour milk into a heavy saucepan. Sprinkle gelatin over milk and stir. Allow gelatin to soften (about 5 minutes). Stir in sugar and heat milk until it simmers; remove from heat. Place yolks in large bowl of electric mixer and beat at medium speed until yolks are thick and lemon colored. Pour hot milk in a thin stream into yolks, beating continuously. Allow milk-egg mixture to cool to room temperature and stir in vanilla. Place in freezer and chill until mixture begins to thicken. Remove from freezer and fold in crushed candy and whipped cream. Spoon into freezer container and place in freezer until it becomes very firm, or at least 6 hours.

Makes about 1 quart.

rum-basted pineapple

For best results be sure to use dark rather than light rum for this recipe.

1	large, fresh pineapple
½ cup	honey
¼ cup	dark rum

Remove rind from pineapple. Halve and remove core. Cut pineapple into 2-inch thick slices. In a bowl, stir together honey and rum. Place pineapple slices in grill basket and place on grill over medium heat. Baste with honey-rum mixture. Cook for 5-7 minutes per side or until lightly browned, turning and basting periodically during cooking. Cool to serve.

Makes 4-6 servings as a dessert or about 8-10 servings as an accompaniment.

plum meringue torte

This dessert is best made on a dry day so that the meringue doesn't get sticky.

4	large egg whites
1⅓ cup	sugar, divided
¼ teaspoon	cream of tartar
6	fresh plums
½ pint	heavy cream
1 teaspoon	vanilla extract
¼ cup	confectioners' sugar

Grease 2 baking sheets and dust with flour.

In large bowl of mixer, beat egg whites with cream of tartar until soft peaks form. Very gradually beat in 1 cup sugar, a tablespoon at a time. Incorporating sugar should take 5-10 minutes. Beat until sugar is dissolved and egg whites are very stiff. Spoon meringue onto baking sheets to form two 9-inch circles and 6 to 8 small puffs.* Bake at 200° F. for 2 hours or until meringues are dry, not browned. Cool.

Meanwhile, slice plums and place in large bowl. Sprinkle with remaining sugar and toss. Allow to stand for at least 1 hour or until sugar dissolves. In another bowl, beat heavy cream with vanilla and confectioners' sugar until stiff.

Torte should be assembled just before serving. Place one meringue on serving plate. Top with ½ plums and ½ whipped cream. Cover with other large meringue, arranging remaining plums carefully on top of second meringue. Decorate with remaining whipped cream and meringue puffs.

Makes one 9-inch torte.

* Meringue layers and puffs can also be shaped by piping stiff egg white out of a pastry bag.

double chocolate cake

This cake is for real chocolate lovers.

½ lb. (2 sticks)	butter or margarine
1 cup	sugar
4	eggs
1 can (16 oz.)	chocolate syrup
1 package (6 oz.)	semi-sweet chocolate bits
1 tablespoon	vanilla extract
2 teaspoons	baking powder
2 cups	flour
1 cup	heavy cream
¼ cup	confectioners' sugar
3 tablespoons	cocoa

In a bowl, cream together butter and sugar. Beat in eggs, one at a time. Add chocolate syrup, chocolate bits and vanilla extract, stirring until well blended. Stir in baking powder and flour and mix thoroughly. Pour into greased 9-inch square baking dish. Bake at 350° F. for 20-30 minutes, being careful not to overbake. Cool and remove from pan.

For filling and topping, pour heavy cream into a bowl. Add confectioners' sugar and cocoa. Beat with mixer until heavy cream is stiff. Split cake horizontally and spread bottom half of cake with half of whipped cream. Cover with top layer of cake and remaining whipped cream.

Makes one 9-inch square cake.

orange-toasted angel cake

Other marmalades or jams can be substituted for the orange flavor.

1	angel cake
1 jar (10 oz.)	orange marmalade
3 tablespoons	butter or margarine, melted

Cut angel cake into about 14 slices. In a bowl, stir together marmalade and butter. Spread each side of cut cake slices with marmalade butter. Place cake slices in grill basket and put on grill over low heat. Cook on each side until cake is toasted.

Makes about 14 servings.

coconut-toasted pound cake

A grilled dessert? The grill is perfect for toasting coconut for this cake.

1 package (10¾ oz.)	frozen pound cake, defrosted
1 package (7 oz.)	flaked coconut
1 can (14 oz.)	sweetened condensed milk

Cut pound cake into ¾-inch thick slices. Put coconut into a shallow bowl. Spread both sides of cake slices with condensed milk and then dip in coconut. Place coated cake slices in grill basket. Place basket on grill over high heat and cook until coconut is toasted on each side.

Makes about 10 servings.

peach cakes

Individual upside down cakes are elegant when piped with whipped cream.

¼ cup	butter or margarine, divided
¼ cup	brown sugar
3	ripe peaches, peeled and halved
1 cup plus 2 tablespoons	cake flour
¾ cup	sugar
6 tablespoons	milk
2	eggs
1¼ teaspoons	baking powder
½ teaspoon	salt
½ teaspoon	vanilla extract

Butter insides of 6 custard cups, using 1 tablespoon butter. Sprinkle insides of cups with brown sugar. Place a peach half, rounded side down in each custard cup; set aside.

Place flour, sugar, milk, eggs, remaining butter, baking powder, salt and vanilla in large bowl of mixer. At low speed, beat until all ingredients are well mixed, scraping bowl with rubber spatula. Beat at medium speed for 5 minutes, scraping bowl occasionally. Pour batter into custard cups over peach halves and spread batter evenly. Place cakes on baking sheet in 375° F. oven for 25-30 minutes. Remove from oven and cool for 10 minutes. Invert custard cups, remove cakes and allow to cool. To serve, garnish with whipped cream, if desired.

Makes 6 servings.

blueberry cream pie

Lemon flavoring in the cream complements the blueberry flavor.

3	egg yolks
⅔ cup	sugar
½ cup	flour
1⅓ cups	milk, scalded
2 tablespoons	lemon juice
1 tablespoon	vanilla extract
2½ teaspoons	grated lemon rind
1	baked 9-inch pie shell
3 cups	fresh blueberries, washed
1 cup	currant jelly

In a large bowl of mixer, beat egg yolks until thick and lemon colored. Slowly beat in sugar and then flour. Pour hot milk slowly into egg yolk mixture while beating continuously. Pour egg-milk mixture into heavy saucepan and place over moderate heat. Cook, stirring continuously, until liquid thickens and cook for an additional 2 minutes. Remove from heat and cool to room temperature. Spoon cream mixture into prepared pie shell. Top with blueberries.

Place currant jelly in a small saucepan and warm over moderate heat. Cook until jelly melts. Spoon over blueberries. Chill pie for 2-3 hours before serving.

Makes one 9-inch pie.

frozen lime soufflé

Sinfully rich and delicious.

4	egg yolks
¾ cup	sugar
½ cup	fresh lime juice
2 teaspoons	grated lime rind
1¼ cups	heavy cream, divided
3 drops	green food coloring
2 tablespoons	confectioners' sugar
1 teaspoon	vanilla extract

In a bowl, beat egg yolks until thick and lemon colored; set aside. In a saucepan, stir together sugar, lime juice and rind. Over moderate heat, cook mixture until sugar is dissolved. Continue cooking until liquid reaches 230° F., using candy thermometer. Remove from heat and very slowly pour hot liquid into egg yolks while beating continuously. In another bowl, beat 1 cup heavy cream until thick; fold into egg yolk mixture. Fold in food coloring. When thoroughly mixed, spoon lime soufflé into 4 serving dishes and place in freezer. Allow to chill for 4-6 hours before serving.

To serve, beat remaining cream with powdered sugar and vanilla until thick. Spoon or pipe cream onto tops of soufflés. Garnish with thin slices of lime.

Makes 4 servings.

peach and blueberry bavarian

Bavarians are an excellent dessert choice with a heavy meal.

2 envelopes (2 tablespoons)	unflavored gelatin
⅓ cup	cold water
1½ cups	peach purée
1 teaspoon	lemon juice
¼ teaspoon	almond extract
4	eggs, separated
½ cup	sugar, divided
1 cup	heavy cream, whipped
½ pint	fresh blueberries, washed and drained

In a small saucepan, soak gelatin in cold water for about 5 minutes or until softened. Place saucepan over low heat and stir until gelatin is dissolved; set aside to cool. In bowl, stir together peach purée, lemon juice and almond extract; set aside. In another bowl, beat 2 egg yolks with 2 tablespoons sugar until thick and lemon colored. Stir in cooled gelatin and peach purée. In a large bowl, beat 4 egg whites until stiff peaks form; slowly beat in sugar until dissolved. Fold beaten whites into peach purée. Then fold in whipped cream. Spoon ⅓ peach mixture into 1½ quart serving dish. Sprinkle with ½ blueberries. Repeat layers, ending with peach mixture. Chill until set. To serve, garnish with peach slices, more blueberries and whipped cream.

Makes 6-8 servings.

marshmallow-baked apples

Try baking dessert right along with dinner and let apples cool while dinner is served.

4	medium apples
¼ cup	packed brown sugar
¼ cup	seedless raisins
¼ teaspoon	ground cinnamon
¼ teaspoon	ground nutmeg
4	marshmallows
	aluminum foil

Remove cores from apples and cut a thin slice of peel from top of apple. In a small bowl, stir together brown sugar, raisins, cinnamon and nutmeg. Fill apple centers with sugar mixture. Top each apple center with marshmallow. Wrap each apple separately in double thickness of aluminum foil. Place apples on Step-Up-Grid and cook, covered, over low heat for 30 minutes.

Makes 4 servings.

peanut butter and chocolate s'mores

A delightful variation of the wonderful outdoor favorite dessert.

12	graham cracker squares
¼ cup	peanut butter
3	milk chocolate candy bars
12	marshmallows
	toasting forks or skewers

Spread 6 graham cracker squares with peanut butter. Top each with squares of milk chocolate. Using fork, toast marshmallows until golden brown. Place 2 toasted marshmallows on top of each square, cover with plain graham cracker squares to make a "sandwich."

Makes 6 servings.

banana boats

Another fireside camping favorite.

6	firm-ripe bananas
4	milk chocolate candy bars
18	marshmallows
	aluminum foil

Remove a thin strip of peel from inside curved surface of banana. Scoop out some of fruit. Line sides of scooped out banana with chocolate squares. Place marshmallows in center of scooped out banana. Place peel back over banana, covering marshmallows. Wrap banana securely with foil. Repeat with other bananas. Place bananas on grill over moderate heat. Cook, covered, for 5-8 minutes. Eat bananas right out of peel.

Makes 6 servings.

bananas alfresco

For an extra special treat, serve bananas with vanilla ice cream.

¼ cup	butter or margarine, melted
3 tablespoons	honey
2 tablespoons	brandy or cognac
2 teaspoons	lemon juice
½ teaspoon	grated lemon rind
6	firm-ripe medium bananas, peeled and halved

In a bowl, stir together butter, honey, brandy, lemon juice and lemon rind. Place bananas in grill basket on grill. Baste with brandy butter. Cook in covered grill over medium to high heat, basting periodically and turning, until bananas are lightly browned.

Makes 6 servings.

floating islands in jamoca cream

Light meringues float in a coffee flavored custard sauce.

3	eggs, separated
⅛ teaspoon	cream of tartar
9 tablespoons	sugar, divided
½ teaspoon	vanilla extract
2½ cups	milk
1 tablespoon	instant coffee
1 cup	light cream
2 tablespoons	coffee-flavored liqueur

In a bowl, beat egg whites at high speed until soft peaks form; beat in cream of tartar. Gradually beat in 5 tablespoons sugar and continue beating until sugar is completely dissolved and meringue forms stiff peaks. Stir in vanilla.

In a shallow fry pan over moderate heat, warm milk to scalding. Using half of meringue at a time, drop meringue in large mounds onto milk. Cook about 5 minutes, turning once. Remove with slotted spoon and drain. Strain remaining milk. Refrigerate poached meringues.

To prepare jamoca cream, beat together egg yolks, remaining sugar, instant coffee and cream. Slowly stir in 1 cup strained milk. Cook in top of double boiler until liquid thickens or about 20 minutes. Add coffee-flavored liqueur; refrigerate. To serve, spoon jamoca cream over poached meringues.

Makes 6 servings.

index